DIALOGUE WITH THE OTHER
THE INTER-RELIGIOUS DIALOGUE

LOUVAIN THEOLOGICAL & PASTORAL MONOGRAPHS

1

DIALOGUE
WITH THE OTHER
The Inter-Religious Dialogue

DAVID TRACY

PEETERS PRESS

LOUVAIN

WILLIAM B. EERDMANS PUBLISHING COMPANY

GRAND RAPIDS, MICHIGAN

ISBN 0-8028-0562-0

Dedicated to

Langdon Gilkey

and

Frank de Graeve,

friends and mentors in inter-religious dialogue
for Christian theology

TABLE OF CONTENTS

ACKNOWLEDGEMENTS IX

PREFACE XI

INTRODUCTION 1

I. MYSTICS, PROPHETS, RHETORICS:
   RELIGION AND PSYCHOANALYSIS 9

   Introduction: Impasse and Exodus 9
   The Rhetoric of Religion: Kenneth Burke 12
   Prophetic Rhetoric and Mystical Rhetoric:
   Freud and Lacan 17

II. THE QUESTION OF CRITERIA FOR INTER-
    RELIGIOUS DIALOGUE:
    ON REVISITING WILLIAM JAMES 27

    Introduction 27
    On Revisiting William James 28
    A Rethinking of Jamesian Criteria:
    Possibility, Coherence, Ethical Consequences 38

III. THE CHALLENGE OF THE ARCHAIC OTHER:
     THE HERMENEUTICS OF MIRCIA ELIADE 48

     The Archaic Other and Christian Theology 48
     Eliade and a Hermeneutics of Creativity in the Inter-
     pretation of Religion 52
     Interpretation Theory:
     Creativity and the Pluralism of Readings 59

IV. THE BUDDHIST-CHRISTIAN DIALOGUE   68

Post-Modernity and Buddhism   68
The Buddhist Challenge of the Self and Transience   74
The Christian and the Buddhist:
Suspicion and Retrieval   79
Can Mystics Read Prophetic Texts Revisited?
The Christian Mystics on the Trinity and the Buddhist
Understanding of Sunyata   83

V. DIALOGUE AND THE PROPHETIC-MYSTICAL
    OPTION   95

Christian Theology and Dialogue   95
The Mystico-Prophetic Traditions of the Religions   100
Narrative and the Interpretation of Christianity   104
The Prophetic Agent in Freedom:
The Mystical-Prophetic Return to History   110

ACKNOWLEDGEMENTS

I am deeply thankful to Professor Raymond Collins of the University of Leuven for his encouragement of this publication and for his fine editorial help and patience at every step. I am also thankful to the University of Leuven, especially Professor Frank de Graeve, Dean Jan Lambrecht, and the trustees of the Dondeyne Lectures for their critiques, and also their kindness and hospitality. I am thankful as well to the president, staff and student body of The American College at Leuven for their generous hospitality during my stay there. My research assistant, Ms. Kathryn Waller, has been invaluable in her assistance on this project. Ms. Judith Lawrence has generously typed and retyped this text on dialogical issues so important to her own religious Vedantist search. I am deeply in their debt.

I wish to thank, as well, the University of Chicago Press for permission to republish the essay on Freud and Lacan which appeared in the collection entitled *Psychoanalysis on Trial*, Françoise Meltzer, editor; and to the *Christian Century* for allowing me to use a part of my essay from their recent series on theologians for the Introduction to this volume; also to St. Mary of the Lake Seminary at Mundelein for the use of part of my lecture on the relevance of William James in the Meyer Lecture at that splendid institution.

My friends, colleagues and students at the University of Chicago and elsewhere continue to be the most generous and critical conversation partners on the issues of this book. To all of them, my deep thanks.

PREFACE:
DIALOGUE AND SOLIDARITY

The present small work is a revised and often expanded version of five lectures delivered at the University of Leuven as the Dondeyne lectures of 1988. I was honored to be invited to be a part of that great university for a short period. My hosts could not have proved more gracious. Their generosity (especially Professor De Graeve) included a critical spirit which helped me, at times, to rethink them anew.

The present work, therefore, is in the form of a series of explorations of aspects of a crucial issue which will transform all Christian theology in the long run: the inter-religious dialogue. The present essays raise distinct but related issues for that dialogue: in the first essay the issue is that of modernity and post-modernity and the relevance of classical "prophetic" and "mystical" models for both religious and secular (Freud and Lacan) discussions. The second essay addresses the question of general criteria for inter-religious dialogue in its philosophical side. The last three essays are more explicitly theological. The third essay provides a theological reading of the significance of the work of the great historian of religions, Mircea Eliade, on the archaic traditions. The fourth essay addresses the Buddhist-Christian dialogue from a Christian theological perspective. The final essay shows the more strictly theological utility of the prophetic-mystical paradigm. As explorations, these essays may help other theologians and philosophers to test the model of dialogue for hermeneutics and the mystical-prophetic model for theology. Indeed, I believe that we are fast approaching the day when it will not be possible to attempt a Christian systematic theology except in serious conversation with the other great ways. But that conviction needs the further test of an explicitly and lengthy systematic theological work. In my own case, this means continuing work on the central Christian question of God viewed from

this prophetic-mystical and inter-religious model. In the meantime, however, some explorations of some basic hermeneutical
terms (e.g., "dialogue") and theological models (e.g., prophetic-
mystical) seem in order.

INTRODUCTION

There are good reasons to understand our period and our needs as more post-modern than modern. Part of the change is clearly cultural: the assumption of cultural superiority of Western modernity is finished. Any thinker who continues to think and write (as many in the modern Western academy still do) as if other cultures either do not exist or exist only as stepping-stones to or pale copies of Western modernity is self-deluding. Most of us now find bizarre those nineteenth century Whig historians like Macaulay with their sublime confidence that true history means what leads up to and finds its glorious culmination in us - the "moderns." A similar fate has overtaken modern liberal philosophical and theological schemas (Hegel, Schleiermacher, Troeltsch, Rahner) on the relationship of Christianity to the other religions.

Another aspect of the change in theology from modernity to post-modernity is facing the new ecclesial situation. The Eurocentric character of Christian theology surely cannot hold in a Christianity that is finally and irreversibly becoming a "world church." That there are now more Anglicans in Africa than in Great Britain, more Presbyterians in South Korea and Taiwan than in Scotland, and will probably be more Roman Catholics at the close of this century in the southern hemisphere than in the northern should give us all pause. No modern theologian can continue to assume that European and North American modes of Christian thought and practice can, even in principle, any longer suffice for an emerging world church.

Another part of the question of post-modernity is less focussed on cultural or ecclesial shifts than on more strictly intellectual problems. Without serious rethinking, the Enlightenment notion of rationality is in grave danger of becoming part of the problem, not the solution. That is even the case for those, like myself, who continue to believe that the very nature of the claims of theology demands public, indeed transcendental or metaphysical explication. This mode of reflection (for Kant, Hegel, Schleiermacher; for Rahner, Tillich, and Whitehead in their competing formulations) always was difficult. But it was also, with great effort, available (viz., by formulating classical metaphysics into modern transcendental terms). The acknowledgement of the role of language (and thereby history) in all understanding united to the acknowledgment of the large role of unconscious factors in all conscious rationality have made those theologically necessary transcendental forms of reflection not impossible, but far, far more difficult to formulate adequately than modern theology (including my own) once believed.

The modern notion of the "self," like the modern notion of "rationality," also needs radical rethinking - especially in new theological anthropologies. The theological language of sin and grace once spoke of a decentered ego with all the force of the most radical French post-modernists. If one doubts this, reread that brilliant, genre-conscious post-modernist (not existentialist), Soren Kierkegaard, on sin, grace, and the decentered Christian self. Even the otherwise happy recovery of the traditions of Christian spirituality in our day are also in danger of becoming further fine tuning, further new peak "experiences," for the omnivorously consuming modern self.

In sum, there is a dark underside to modern thought, including modern theology. Anyone who senses this problem at all is likely to attempt one or another form of post-modern theology. Some forms of this will prove straightforwardly anti-modern: as in the profound but disturbing reflections of Alexander Solzhenitsyn, the Augustinian pessimism pervading the theology and restorationist policies of Josef Cardinal Ratzinger or a good deal of the rhetoric (if, happily, not the practices) of some of the neo-Barthian theologies. Other forms will prove more clearly post-modern: as in the powerful reflections of Gustavo Guttiérez on the need for contemporary theology to face the reality of the "non-person" of the oppressed in the massive global suffering surrounding us as distinct from modern theology's more typical concern with the "non-believer;" as in the many alternative forms of post-modern theologies in feminist, womanist, African-American, and global liberationist struggles and theologies. Still others will embrace post-modernity in its most decentering, deconstructive forms so fully that "a-theologies" are born to announce, yet again, that the "death of God" has finally found its true hermeneutical home.

"May you live in interesting times," we are reminded, is an ancient Chinese curse. Unfortunately, the choice of when to live is not ours, but only how. This is not a time when Western culture needs one last burst of overweening, indeed hubristic, self-confidence masking self-absorption and newfound insecurity. It is a time when we all need to face the strong claims to attention of other cultures and of the other, subjugated, forgotten, and marginalized traditions in Western culture itself. We also need to face the ambiguous otherness within our own psyches (Freud - Lacan) and traditions. The last great attempt to salvage modernity - indeed so great an attempt that it bears all the marks of classical Greek tragedy - was Husserl's *Crisis of the European Sciences*. After that, the deluge.

Amidst the often conflicting strategies for rethinking our situation and thereby rethinking our pluralistic and ambiguous heritage, the emergence of contemporary hermeneutics can prove of some aid. From the exposés of the illusions of modern conscious rationality by Freud, Marx, and Nietzsche through contemporary feminist theory, modernity has been forced to rethink its Enlightenment heritage on both reason and the self in increasingly radical, that is, post-modern, de-centering forms. Central here has been the post-modern rereadings of Freud, Marx, and Nietzsche themselves, especially by feminist thinkers. Or consider Walter Benjamin's willingness to rethink the classic traditions he so loved, now guided by the hermeneutical acknowledgement that "every great work of civilization is at the same time a work of barbarism." Consider Foucault's noble attempts to rethink and retrieve the "subjugated" knowledge of our own past. In every case of serious post-modern thought, radical hermeneutical rethinking recurs. It is little wonder that the most marginalized groups of our heritage - mystics, hysterics, the mad, fools, apocalyptic groups, dissenters of all kind, avant-garde artists - now claim the attention of many post-modern searchers for an alternative version of a usable past.

The emergence of a hermeneutical consciousness is clearly a part of this cultural shift. For hermeneutics lives or dies by its ability to take history and language seriously, to allow the other (whether person, event, or text) to claim our attention as other, not as a projection of our present fears, hopes and desires. The deceptively simple hermeneutical model of dialogue is one attempt to be faithful to this shift from modern self to post-modern other. For however often the word is bandied about, dialogue remains a rare phenomenon in anyone's experience. Dialogue demands the intellectual, moral, and, at the limit, religious ability to struggle to hear another and to respond. To respond critically, and even suspiciously when necessary, but to respond only in dialogical relationship to a real, not a projected other.

For example, my own attempts, in the last ten years, to enter into interreligious dialogues have revealed the same kind of hermeneutical need to attend to a real, not a projected, other. Consider the crucial need to rethink the Christian relationship to indigenous traditions (still often misnamed "pagans" or even "primitives") by facing the history of Christian projections upon and oppression of those traditions in Europe, Asia, Africa, Oceania, and the Americas. Consider the needs of Jewish-Christian dialogue in a post-Holocaust situation. How can we pretend to take history with theological seriousness and then ignore the Holocaust? If we do ignore it, then we should either admit the bankruptcy of all theological talk on history as the locus of divine action and human responsibility or admit that we will only allow the "good" parts of our history prove worthy of theological reflection.

With the Jew and the so-called pagan, the Christian in dialogue (which demands, in practice, solidarity) needs to face the constant Christian temptation to project a Christian consciousness upon the other. Both the "pagan" and the "Jew" have too often served as the projected other of "Christian" self-understanding. With the Buddhist, the need is to face, at last, not a projected other but this great other tradition with its profound vision of ultimate reality as emptiness (*sunyata*). Buddhists speak and live that vision so persuasively that, in first meeting them, Christian theologians, like myself, are hurled into a state of such initial confusion that it bears all the marks of an experience of the *mysterium fascinans et tremendum*. It is the dialogue with Buddhists that has forced me to rethink theologically the more radically apophatic mystics of the tradition, especially Meister Eckhart.

It is the dialogue with Buddhists, as a second example, that has forced me to see how even so classic a Christian witness as Francis of Assisi can be allowed to speak anew to all Christians concerned to establish new relationships to all creatures (not only humans) and thereby to the whole earth. This may seem a strange claim, for Francis of Assisi is the one Christian saint whom all Westerners profess to love even if most quietly continue to view him as a kind of holy fool who somehow wandered off the pages of Dostoyevsky.

But Francis was, in fact — as Buddhists see clearly — a Christian of such excess and challenge to ordinary, even good, Christian ways of understanding all of God's creation as beloved that we still cannot see him clearly. We have not yet, in Christian theological dialogue, taken even Francis of Assisi seriously.

Examples of the results of how dialogue with the other also makes one radically rethink one's own heritage could easily be multiplied beyond the examples of Eckhart and Francis (consider the women mystics or the Shakers). It is my experience, and it has become my conviction, that the "hermeneutical turn" in theology is a difficult and demanding practice just as it is a necessarily complex theory.

If we are to hear one another once again, then dialogue and the solidarity amidst the differences and conflicts which dialogue may demand is our best present hope. There is no escape from the insight which modernity most feared: there is no innocent tradition (including modernity), no innocent classic (including the scriptures) and no innocent reading (including this one). My hope is in genuinely dialogical thought accompanied by real solidarity in action. Otherwise we are back where we began: with officially exorcised but practically dominant programs of Western and modern stories of progress; with monological forms of rationality and increasingly brittle notions of a self seemingly coherent but actually possessive and consumerist; with "others" present, if at all, only as projections of our modern selves, our desires, wants, needs.

It has also been my experience as it has become my conviction that sometimes the best road to hermeneutical retrievals of tradition is through critique and suspicion. One route to retrieval is the facing of the disturbing otherness within ourselves and our traditions as well as the reality of others waiting, no longer patiently, to speak. It is no small matter, I believe, that there are now many "others" who do theology in ways very different, even conflictually other, from my own white, male, middle class, and academic reflections on a hermeneutics of dialogue and a praxis of solidarity. They bespeak critiques, suspicions, and retrievals of the Christian theological heritage which I too need to hear far better than I have to date. What seems to me to unite so many of these new voices is not a theory of hermeneutics, much less a revised correlational method for theology. Rather it is a new hermeneutical practice which actualizes that theory and that method better than many of the theorists do.

This new hermeneutical practice become living theology can best be described as "mystical-prophetic." The hyphen is what compels my interest. For these classic religious types, the prophet and the mystic, are just as much figures of religious excess as they are figures of theological conflict. How then can we think such two different modes of religious otherness together? That is the question towards which much serious theology today strives. In my own former work (viz., in *The Analogical Imagination*) I tried to rethink the traditional Christian theological dialectic of sacrament and word as the more primordial religious dialectic of "manifestation" and "proclamation." I continue to believe that such a religious dialectic is at the heart of Christianity. But I now see more clearly - thanks to the inter-religious dialogue, the voices of the new theologies allied with the welcome recovery of spirituality within theology - that, in practice and thereby in theory, this pervasive religious dialectic of manifestation and proclamation is best construed theologically as mystical-prophetic. Hence this small book as one test of that wider effort.

MYSTICS, PROPHETS, RHETORICS:
RELIGION AND PSYCHOANALYSIS

Introduction: Impasse and Exodus

Perhaps we have finally reached the end of the more familiar discussions of Freud and religion. Surely we do not need another round of theologians showing the "ultimate concern" in the works of Freud. Nor do we really need psychoanalysts announcing, once again, that religions are finally, indeed totally, illusion. Orthodox religionists have long since noted the many obvious religious analogues in Freud's work: the founding of the orthodox church, the purges of the heretical "Gnostic" Jung and the "Anabaptist" Adler, the debates over the translations of the sacred texts and their proper modes of interpretation. Orthodox Freudian psychoanalysts have amply demonstrated the psychological realities embedded in many religious phenomena: the obsessional nature of some religious rituals, the over-determined character of all religious symbols, and, even, at times, the original patricide in totemic and monotheistic religions alike. In each case, the list could easily be extended. But should it? Or might it not prove more fruitful to reflect on the clashing rhetorical strategies in this clash of claims? Each rhetorical strategy has now proved its usefulness and its limits. These limits are now clear to everyone except those religionists who cannot help finding religion anywhere a serious concern is at stake (i.e., literally everywhere) and those psychoanalysts incapable of noticing anything in religion except neurosis. On both these latter analyses, everything is finally the same thing. The only rhetorical strategy approved is a myth of the eternal return of more of the same.

Behind these two exhausted rhetorical moves lie two exhausted rhetorics: on the one side, a rhetoric of "pure science" that is neither pure nor notably scientific; on the other side, a rhetoric of "pure religion" that makes all religions so pure, so loving, so nice that no recognizable historical expression of religion fits the portrait. Even the entry of philosophy can often increase the problem rather than, as promised, resolve it. For any philosophy which effectively denies the reality of the unconscious in favor of its usual claims for consciousness and pure reason can hardly help. Sometimes, the philosophies straightforwardly deny that the unconscious means anything other than the pre-conscious (Sartre and de Beauvoir). At other times, more fruitful strategies are forged: as when philosophers admit the challenge of psychoanalysis and then see what philosophical analysis might have to say in return (Ricoeur and Cavell).[1] This second kind of move does lead to a new mutual challenge of psychoanalysis and philosophy: at least when Ricoeur's Hegel (rather than Kant) or Cavell's Wittgenstein (rather than Russell) helps the post-Freudian philosopher speak back in the presence of, rather than by means of the denial of, the unconscious.

Theologians have an even more difficult task than the philosophers. They too are tempted to deny any connection between those two notoriously over-determined phenomena: the unconscious and religion. They, too, may prefer to rush back to safer rhetorical ground—the endless Western debate on "theism" and "atheism." In arguments for or against the existence of God, after all, there is no unconscious and there often may as well be no historical religion either. On this question of God, all is determined, nothing is over-determined. Here a consciousness free of any unconscious can have one last fling—proving or disproving "God." Has "God" become the one clear and distinct idea left? Alternatively, "God" may become, for many, the favorite candidate for the "transcendental signified"—briefly mentioned before everyone rushes on to more interesting candidates like the "subject." The problem in all this is that God, religiously construed, is not merely the problem of consciousness

---

[1] Paul Ricoeur, *Freud and Philosophy: An Essay in Interpretation* (New Haven: Yale University Press, 1970).

but also a question of the unconscious. Mystics (and Lacan) know this. Most philosophers, theologians, and psychoanalysts do not. This is what makes Lacan's reading of Freud theologically interesting. At last the question of God is not simply who can produce the best philosophical argument on the implications of consciousness. Nor is the question who (Peter Gay or Hans Küng) can give the best explanation for the fact that Freud's atheism was chronologically pre-psychoanalytical.[2]

The first question is not even what is the referent of all this God-talk—or, for that matter, all this talk of the unconscious. Rather the Lacanian reading of Freud suggests a more interesting question: what is the rhetorical character of Lacan's reading of Freud if construed as the clash of two familiar religious rhetorics, the prophetic and the mystical? This new question, to be sure, has its own problems. It can seem to assume that we are all clear on the conflicting psychoanalytic rhetorics of Freud and Lacan, which, despite some fine studies, we are not.[3] The question can also seem to assume that we are all clear on the rhetoric of religion, which, again despite some good studies, we are not.[4] Despite these difficulties, the new question does have one advantage: it allows all rhetorical analysts to suspend the question of the referent, if any, of all this religious God-talk and simply analyze the necessary emergence of "god-terms" in all rhetorics, whether explicitly religious ones like those of the classic prophets and mystics or classically secular ones like Freud's and Lacan's.

To clarify the question itself, the following steps seem appropriate: first, analyze the "rhetoric of religion" and the emergence of "god-terms" in all rhetorics via Kenneth Burke (the best

[2] Peter Gay, *A Godless Jew: Freud, Atheism and the Making of Psychoanalysis* (New Haven: Yale University Press, 1987); Hans Küng, *Freud and the Problem of God* (New Haven: Yale University Press, 1979).

[3] Patrick J. Mahoney, *Freud as a Writer* (New Haven: Yale University Press, 1987); Samuel Weber, *The Legend of Freud* (Minneapolis: The University of Minnesota Press, 1982).

[4] Representative studies may be found in Robert Alter and Frank Kermode, eds., *The Literary Guide to the Bible*, (Cambridge: Harvard University Press, 1987).

rhetorical analysis of religion available to date);[5] second, compli-
cate Burke's general rhetoric of religion by introducing the more
specific and contrasting rhetorics of the two classic religious
types—the prophet and the mystic; third, see whether the classic
conflict between prophetic and mystical rhetorics may illuminate
the analogous clash between the rhetorics of Freud and Lacan.
On this reading, the question "Does Lacan read Freud accurately?" becomes uncannily similar to the familiar theological question: can a mystic read correctly the prophetic texts she or he
claims to be interpreting? In neither case is the answer self-
evident. But by recalling the conflicting rhetorics of prophet and
mystic, we may find a new way to suggest what is really at stake
in the rhetoric of psychoanalysis itself become the conflicting
rhetorics of Freud and Lacan.

The Rhetoric of Religion: Kenneth Burke

Kenneth Burke has been well described as an "analytical and
moralizing therapist of the human mess."[6] Burke, as a good
rhetorician, is principally interested in changing fundamental
attitudes. We can, he urges, transform our temptations to scientism, romanticism, absolutism, monomania, and so forth into a
fundamental attitude which, while contemplating generic necessities, can allow us to "dance with tears in our eyes." One can
name this Burkean "fundamental attitude," as Burke does, his
own "neo-Stoic" resignation. One can also understand it (as I
tend to do) as tragi-comic: that is, the "representative anecdote"
for Burke is closer to the *Oresteia*: three tragedies followed by a
satyr play. This, at least, is what the rhetorical structure of *The
Rhetoric of Religion* is. Since that work rhetorically analyzes our
most fundamental attitudes it can serve as a good clue to Burke's
own ultimate vision as a tragi-comic one. We can use Burke's

[5] Kenneth Burke, *The Rhetoric of Religion* (Berkeley: The University of
California Press, 1970).

[6] In an unpublished paper by David Smigelskis for the Seminar in Rhetoric of
the Committee on the Analysis of Ideas and Methods (1984).

rhetoric of persuasion on generic necessities in the same way we (most of us, I suspect) have learned to use other great "analytical and moralizing therapists of the human mess" (Aeschylus, Augustine, Calvin, Edwards, Freud, Marx, Nietzsche, *et. al.*). All these "masters of suspicion" do provide persuasive analyses of the unnerving presence of certain generic necessities in the human mess. More exactly, there are certain fundamental attitudes in human beings which are frightening (and deserve some good analysis and sometimes, as Freud knew, even moralizing).[7] There are good persuasive reasons why, in concrete cases (e.g., Freud's *Dora*), such analyses do illuminate what the problem may be. In many of our "masters of suspicion" the analysis can quickly become a totalizing interpretation of the "human situation."

But exactly here Burke's own candidate for a generic necessity is illuminating: namely, the drive to perfection seemingly incumbent upon all language use of any terministic screen. This Burkean rhetorical tool does analytically illuminate the totalizing temptation in all positions including the masters of suspicion and retrieval; the rhetoric of deliberation on a multiplicity of goods; the absolutisms endemic to religion; the scientism endemic to science; the imperialism endemic to rhetoric; the monomania endemic to most insights - recall René Girard in *Violence and the Sacred* yielding to a kind of monomaniacal totalizing of a good insight.[8]

The heart of Burke's tragi-comic vision claims that endemic to human beings (and best disclosed in their language) is a drive to perfection. This drive, when analyzed, discloses a remarkable ambiguity: our creativity is dependent on this drive (and it is the best thing about us). At the very same time, we are "rotten with perfection." We turn every insight into a total system, every

---

[7] On this side of Freud, see Philip Rieff, *Freud: The Mind of the Moralist* (Chicago: The University of Chicago Press, 1979).

[8] Rene Girard, *Violence and the Sacred* (Baltimore: Johns Hopkins University Press, 1977).

creative activity (art, science, religion become romanticism, scientism, absolutism; technology becomes *Helhaven* on the moon). What then, in this situation, can we do? We can analyze this entelchy (enter his two rhetorical strategies, dramatism and logology).[9] We can accept our fate by accepting *this* generic necessity. We can cultivate a fundamental attitude that is tragi-comic (Freud-Lacan?) and, by that cultivation, we can "purify war" by turning war into, not peace (impossible on this perspective), but conversation, perspective by incongruity, irony, or, as Burke prefers, "dancing with tears in our eyes."

If we are persuaded on the need for a rhetoric of persuasion on fundamental attitudes like Burke's, then our problem becomes a familiar one: how persuasive is Burke's account of this generic necessity (the drive to perfection) and how does it relate to alternative accounts of generic necessities (Augustine, Marx, Freud, Nietzsche, etc.)? What is unfamiliar and significant about this new kind of Burkean rhetorical analysis of perfection, however, is that even if Burke's account of the drive to perfection is persuasive, he has also built into his choice what other accounts of the radical ambiguity of the "human mess" possess less clearly: namely, the very necessity and ambiguity of perfection as the key generic necessity leads one to be suspicious of the key itself. This aspect of Burke's rhetoric of persuasion is, I think, more subtle (and, therefore, more persuasive?) than many alternatives. His major competitor for this particular subtlety would seem to be Nietzsche - at least the "new Nietzsche," that honorary French thinker of différence. This is probably the reason why Burke is

---

[9] For two studies of Burke, see Frank Lentricchia, *Criticism and Social Change* (Chicago: The University of Chicago Press, 1983); Williams H. Ruerhert, *Kenneth Burke and the Drama of Human Relatives* (Berkeley and Los Angeles: The University of California Press, 1982). For the present analysis, besides *The Rhetoric of Religion*, the central texts of Burke would be: *The Philosophy of Literary Form: Studies in Symbolic Action* (Berkeley and Los Angeles: The University of California Press, 1957); *A Grammar of Motives* (New York: Prentice-Hall, 1945); *A Rhetoric of Motives* (Berkeley and Los Angeles: The University of California Press, 1969).

sometimes made an honorary member of the "new rhetoric." If Nietzsche can become French, why not Kenneth Burke?

The *Rhetoric of Religion* becomes the *non-plus ultra* text of all Burke's rhetorics of persuasion on attitudes. Burke is interested in religions because he is interested in attitudes: "The subject of religion falls under the head of *rhetoric* in the sense that rhetoric is the art of *persuasion*, and religious cosmogonies are designed, in the last analysis, as exceptionally thoroughgoing modes of persuasion. To persuade men towards certain acts, religions would form the kinds of attitude which prepare men for such acts. In order to plead for such attitudes as persuasively as possible, the religions always ground their exhortations (to themselves and others) in statements of the widest and deepest possible scope, concerning the authorship of men's motives."[10]

The first two sentences of this crucial passage seem a clear illustration of Burke's enterprise: if rhetoric has to do with a persuasion to action by changing attitudes, then study that phenomenon which changes attitudes most "thoroughly." This is also the key to Burke's shift from considering "poetic" language as the privileged instance of "language as symbolic action" to "religious" language as the privileged instance of "language as such as motive." Religions are more "thorough going" than poetic speech or dramas. They will not simply cancel out what we learned under the rubric "dramatism" but (by their greater abstractness, generality, and thoroughness) they will move the analysis of rhetorical persuasion to more general, more thorough, fundamental attitudes.

Hence we need a new form of analysis of this "ultimate" rhetoric of persuasion: namely, a new rhetorical enterprise named logology. But here some confusion enters: logology will be a rhetorical discipline that will study words-about-words and since words about words disclose a drive to perfection in all words, then we must study *words*-about-God (god terms). Is that why we need a rhetoric of religion? Well, not quite - for it seems that it is

---

[10] Kenneth Burke, *The Rhetoric of Religion*, p. V.

not so much religion we need to study but "theology." Why? It cannot simply be that theology is more verbal than religion, although that is true and Burke mentions it. For Burke's earlier dramatism already taught us (did it not?) not to have a simple contrast between words and actions.

Something else is at stake - and something, as Burke likes to say, "complicated." My guess is this: religions help Burke to reflect principally on a radicalized, generalized rhetoric of persuasion to attitudes; theologies help Burke to reflect principally on radicalized, generalized analysis of generic necessities (namely, the drive to perfection in all language.)

Only logology can move our concerns past all "privileged cases" (whether drama, poetry or religion) to a study of words as such (words about words). But we should still search for some "privileged case" that can at least initiate our analysis. Choose, then, "words about God," god-terms. An analysis of "words about God" reveals a generic necessity to all words, language, namely, the drive to perfection. God-language (for radical monotheists, at least), is perfection-language - recall Charles Hartshorne on the logic of perfection in God-language.[11] But the "early" Burke already argued that the peculiarity of human beings is that, as "symbolic animals," human beings are language-beings. They learn by learning negatives (the prophetic negatives "thou shall not") in order to create. Once they learn that they cannot stop going to the end of the line - the line of the widest possible generalization, the most perfect language for the truly creative act, to god-terms. (God *as* "Pure Act;" Genesis as Pure Act, as origin determining the whole cycle of terms: creation-covenant-guilt-redemption which seem narrative-temporal but are synchronic-systemic.)[12]

We are driven to perfect our creations, our language. We are driven, wherever we begin, to god-terms. The basic necessity for the symbolic animal is to speak, to learn negatives, to create and *not* to stop. Perfection is our *telos* - which seems to mean,

---

[11] Charles Hartshorne, *The Logic of Perfection.*
[12] See Burke's unusual analysis of Genesis here in *The Rhetoric of Religion.*

paradoxically, that end *is* origin. Once we acknowledge that non-*telos*, - *telos* via rhetorical analysis of privileged god-terms, we learn a generic necessity (our necessary drive to perfection) that becomes a vision of "transcendence" informing our move back to history ("the cave?"). Our freedom, as true freedom is determined (re-enter Calvin, Spinoza, and Freud). Even "symbol" and "animality" (those two generic necessities of the "symbol-making animal") seem to meet as our creative, symbolic power of words drives us to a perfection language which returns history to nature, freedom to necessity, and narratives like Augustine's *Confessions* and *Genesis* to an a-temporal cycle of terms. End is origin.[13]

Prophetic Rhetoric and Mystical Rhetoric: Freud and Lacan

Burke's analysis shows, in rhetorical terms, the further meaning of Hegel's or Hartshorne's philosophical interpretations of God-language as perfection-language. A rhetorical analysis, moreover, has one advantage over more purely dialectical enterprises: it opens to an acknowledgment of the reality of the unconscious in the words we use and the god-terms we inevitably employ. The "rottenness of perfection" position of Burke suggests at best ambiguity and, at the limit, over-determination in all our conscious "god-terms".

Burke's properly general analysis of the rhetoric of religion as a drive to perfection language needs, however, further specificity. For religious languages arrive in two basic forms: the rhetoric of the prophet and the rhetoric of the mystic.[14] First, the prophet: the prophet hears a word that is not his own. It is Other. It

---

[13] A Burkean conclusion remarkably similar to that of Mircea Eliade on cosmogonic myths; see Mircea Eliade, *The Myth of the Eternal Return* (Princeton: Princeton University Press, 1957) and *The Sacred and the Profane: The Nature of Religion* (New York: Harper, 1957).

[14] The same contrast can be made through a distinction between "manifestation" and "proclamation"; see Paul Ricoeur, "Manifestation and Proclamation," *The Journal of the Blaisdall Institute 12* (Winter 1978) or my own reformulation in *The Analogical Imagination: Christian Theology and the Culture of Pluralism* (New York: Crossroad, 1981).

disrupts consciousness, actions, deliberations. It demands expression through the prophet. The prophet is not his own person; something else speaks here. Only on behalf of that Other may the prophet presume to speak her warnings, interruptive proclamations, predictions and promises. Driven by a perfection-language needing god-terms to disclose this Other who or which speaks through the prophet, she or he cannot but speak. The others ordinarily do not want to listen. If matters get bad enough (and they usually will, given the "human mess"), others may begin to listen: first to the puzzling words of the prophet; then to the disturbing words of the Other in those words; then to the word of that Other in themselves. Some listen, some come for help, some are healed. Their healing will rarely prove a full recovery but, like Peter Brown's Augustine[15] or Freud's Dora, more like a continuous convalescence. For consolation from all sorrow they must go elsewhere—to those who deny the Other. For the rhetoric of the prophet can only listen and help them hear the words of the Other in themselves.

Prophets have good reason to be discouraged about how few will listen. "Let him who has ears to hear, hear" is not a rhetoric that rings with the assurance of success. Sometimes the prophets reflect their own fury at this Other who insists on speaking in them: witness the lamentations of Jeremiah and many of the letters of Freud. At other times this fury will disclose itself in the gaps, the fissures, the repressions of the prophet's own too clear prose.[16] At still other times, the prophets (or their successors) will yield to more reflective moods. They will face the fact that people seem to demand, not a word of the Other, but a consolation that cannot be given. They will note that the prophetic word is also "rotten with perfection." *Ecclesiastes*, that oddest of biblical

[15] Peter Brown, *Augustine of Hippo* (Berkeley: The University of California Press, 1970).

[16] For a good example here, see Françoise Meltzer, "The Uncanny Rendered Canny: Freud's Blind Spot in Meeting Hoffmann's Sandman," Sander Gilman, ed., *International Psychoanalytic Theory* (New York: Brunner Mazel, 1982).

books, is, rhetorically, that kind of work; so is *Civilization and Its Discontents.*

Freud was not a conquistador. His rhetoric was that of a prophet. Through his words—as clear, definite and, at the same time, self-interruptive as those of Amos—some Other spoke. Like all prophets, he would not let his prose indulge itself in what, for the prophet, must be viewed as the obscure and bizarre allegories of an apocalypticist nor the weird, uncanny obfuscations of the mystic. He needed words that allowed the unconscious to speak and words persuasive enough to entice others to listen to that Other. But only clear, everyday words rendered with classic humanist restraint could allow that Other to be heard in such manner that others might hear and be persuaded. Freud called his god-term *Logos*—not mystery, not Other, not law.[17] He called his discipline scientific. Science was for him, as for most in his period, the longed-for language of perfection after other languages (art, religion, myth) had failed. He often wanted to believe that his rhetoric was purely scientific. Happily, it was also something else:[18] a rhetoric of corrigibility, clarity, and a search for evidence that does resemble science; a prose whose subtlety and restraint does resemble Goethe; yet both that scientific and humanist prose was finally an interruptive one—constantly interrupted, even disrupted, by the voice of the Other. By trying to render that subversive reality of the unconscious into seemingly scientific and humanist prose, Freud's powerful prophetic rhetoric challenged the ordinary prose of science and humanism alike as surely as the classic prophets' rhetoric, however clear and definite, smashed against the iconic proses, the idols, of the people. The prose becomes more and more polyvalent as it turns upon others and itself through the strange stories it narrates so well and the even stranger fissures and lapses it harbors within its own definiteness.

[17] Sigmund Freud, *The Future of an Illusion* (New York: Norton, 1975).

[18] A reinterpretation of Wittgenstein's remarks on Freud leads to a similar conclusion—as argued well in the dissertation-in-progress of Charles Elder (The University of Chicago).

Finally every word, including every word about words, becomes not merely ambiguous and polyvalent, as Burke sees, but over-determined and disseminating—as Freud saw. The very material reality of these words of the Other invades all words—even the scientific words of Freud, the humanistic prose, the care and search for clarity and harmony. In that sense, Freud's persuasive prophetic rhetoric becomes, in his greatest texts, something like a kabbalistic palimpsest filled with words whose very materiality are the central clues to the revealing and concealing of the Other-in-words.[19]

Freud may have wished to produce a purely scientific body of work. In one sense, he did. But he also produced something more—a prophetic rhetoric of persuasion to the Other. He may have called his god "Logos" but he was no neo-Platonist. As a "godless Jew," he consciously ignored the prophets, the rabbis, and the kabbalists only to have their most typical rhetorical strategies emerge in his own German-Greek humanist prose. Even as a Greek, he was odd: he praised *Logos* as much as any Platonist in the first academy but often wandered out of Plato's academy to attend to the forbidden texts of Aeschylus and Sophocles. Like so many Greeks of the classical age, he also seemed to long for some other wisdom, some other god-term than *Logos*. As Herodotus makes clear, for the classical Greek imagination, Egypt became the land where an other wisdom—the wisdom of the Other?—may lie. Thus did the great Greek-Jew Freud often travel in his imagination to Egypt. Even Moses must become an Egyptian. Then his "murder" by the Jews and his puzzling Exodus from the homeland of Egypt might finally be

---

[19] This textual resemblance is not dependent on historical influence. The latter claim seems far more dubious. For the claim itself, see David Bakan, *Sigmund Freud and the Jewish Mystical Tradition* (Boston: Beacon, 1975). For rhetorical analyses of the classical "Jewish" ways of reading texts, see Susan Handelman, *The Slayer of Moses: The Emergence of Rabbinic Interpretation in Modern Literary Theory* (Albany: State University of New York Press, 1982) and Harold Bloom, *Kabbalah and Criticism* (New York: Seabury, 1975).

intelligible.[20] Even Plato and Pythagoras—with their god Logos—must have learned from Egypt.

Freud's god-term was not "God"—and surely not the radically monotheistic God of Ahknaton and Moses. It was also not really Logos, nor was it the radically monotheistic science of the *philosophes* and the nineteenth century scientists. His god-term was not even the Unconscious. Indeed, the discovery of the unconscious teaches once again the most ancient of Jewish commands: the god-term should remain unnameable; it is not to be named. All we have are the words of the Other: material words to be deciphered and even then only partially understood by this non-believing prophet and this non-observant kabbalist. What Freud sometimes wanted—from his god-term *Logos*—was a stabilizing rhetoric of the topics. What he received—from the Other in the unconscious—was a radically destabilizing prophetic rhetoric of the tropes. Jacques Lacan spotted this secret of the prophet with all the self-confidence of a mystic assuming that only he could understand what the prophet really meant. For mystics, unlike prophets, have no hesitation in allowing the destabilizing discourse of the Other the fullest sway.

Mystical religious discourse is startlingly different from prophetic discourse. Both are driven by an impulse towards perfection in their words about the Word. Both seem driven by an Other who speaks. For the prophet, the Other is Word acknowledged in a word of proclamation ("Thus says the Lord") that disrupts the prophet's own consciousness and disseminates the ego.[21] For the prophet, that Word, as One, demands a new center of unity beyond the ego. For the prophet is not her or his own person. The prophet, as responsible to the *fascinans et tremendum* reality of the Word, must become a new, responsible self—responsible to others, to history, to the cosmos, because made a responsible self

[20] Sigmund Freud, *Moses and Monotheism* (New York: Vintage, 1967), especially pages 3-72.

[21] For some studies here, see James Luther Mays and Paul J. Achtemeier, eds., *Interpreting the Prophets* (Philadelphia: Fortress, 1987) and Robert Alter and Frank Kermode, *The Literary Guide to the Bible*, pp. 165-234.

by the Other-as-Word.[22] Only by losing the self can a new self be gained. The Word, the god-term named God, must remain Other or else the other in the new, responsible self cannot speak. The great Western monotheistic traditions (Judaism, Christianity, Islam) live by and through this prophetic rhetoric on the one God and the newly unified, responsible, othered self.

For many Eastern mystical traditions this prophetic discourse on God and the self is a symptom of the deeper problem, not an expression of the solution. For the most radical of these traditions, the Chan and Zen forms of Mahayana Buddhism, the prophet clings to a double illusion: that there is an Other that is Other (and thereby to be worshipped and trusted as "God") and that there is a self at all. Only by letting go of this form of primary ignorance (*avidya*) can all clinging and ultimately all desire cease. There is no "God" and there is no "self." There is not even a real *nirvana* and a real *samsara*. We must also not cling to enlightenment itself. For *nirvana* and *samsara* are one— one (more exactly, "not two") in their emptiness, but not one in the union/encounter of the prophet and the covenanting God, not one in the radical identity of the Hindu Shankara's Brahman-beyond-God and Atman-beyond-the-self.

This most radical of Buddhist mystical rhetorics illustrates, by its very radicality, certain crucial features of all mystical traditions: even the usually marginalized strands of mysticism in the Western prophetic traditions, even that of Buddhism's greatest opponent—the Vedantic tradition of Hinduism, even that of the return of the Other in the "other-power" of Pure Land Buddhism. For all mystics want to say something more than the prophet is willing to say—and say it as what the prophet really meant or should have meant. Zen Buddhist rhetoric does have certain affinities with some Western rhetorics—but not, I believe, with either Freud or Lacan. Rather Zen Buddhist rhetorics is far

---

[22] See H. Richard Niebuhr, *Radical Monotheism and Western Culture* (New York: Harper & Row, 1960).

more like Derrida's. Indeed Nagarjuna and Derrida,[23] with all their differences, are natural allies with their insistence on non-presence, their attempts to undo dialectic dialectically, their disclosures of the radical instability of all linguistic attempts to secure a determinate meaning. Even the "indeterminate" will not suffice: Derrida's *différence* is not a candidate for a new transcendental category; Nagarjuna's no-self is not a doctrine for it neither exists nor does not exist; both discover the play of Nothingness behind the mere nihility of all tragic humanisms obsessed with a "self."

However, this kind of radical Zen and deconstructionist discourse does not really fit the kind of rhetoric in the destabilizing tropes of Lacan. For an analogy to Lacan, we must return to the Western monotheistic traditions and note a peculiar kind of apophatic mysticism emerging there. The rhetoric of the great Western love-mystics (Bernard of Clairvaux, Teresa of Avila, John of the Cross) may attract a Julia Kristeva with her post-Lacan and anti-Derrida semiotic rhetoric of a subject-in-process in transference love.[24] But all—literally all—that interests Lacan in Teresa of Avila is her *jouissance* and the excess and radical negations it discloses.[25] But that all is everything and the clue of the radically apophatic, but not Zen, rhetoric of Lacan.

Mystics in prophetic traditions (as all Western monotheisms are) always have problems. Unless they are very cautious in their marginalized place, some prophet (or more likely, some hierarch with prophetic pretensions) will accuse them of betrayal. Where is the God of the prophets in the Godhead-beyond-God of Meister Eckhart? Where are the energetics of Freud's unconscious in the

[23] See Robert Magliola, *Derrida on the Mend* (West Lafayette, IN: Purdue University Press, 1984). This difference may also help to interpret the differences of Lacan and Derrida. On the latter, see Barbara Johnson, "The Frame of Reference: Poe, Lacan, Derrida", in *The Critical Difference: Essays in the Contemporary Rhetoric of Reading* (Baltimore: Johns Hopkins University Press, 1980).

[24] Julia Kristeva, *Tales of Love* (New York: Columbia University Press, 1987).

[25] Jacques Lacan and the école freudienne, "God and the *Jouissance* of the Woman", in *Feminine Sexuality* (New York: W.W. Norton, 1982), pp. 137-49.

linguistic Unconscious of Lacan? Where is the radically monotheistic God and the responsible self in the apophatic Jewish,
Christian, and Muslim mystics? Where is Freud's god *Logos* and
where is the ego in the uncontrollable prose and the unnerving
tropes of Lacan? Have the Western apophatic mystics betrayed
the prophets for Neo-Platonism? Has Lacan betrayed Freud for
Hegel and Heidegger?

At first, it may seem that monotheism is still honored by the
mystics and a scientific Logos is honored by Lacan. For the
mystic will try to reduce the world portrayed in the Bible to its
most basic elements (God, world, soul) in order to observe their
structural relationships. Mystics almost always have some basic
grammar as their first move. Even Buddhists have the language of
"co-dependent origination." Even Eckhart possesses a highly
peculiar grammar of analogy.[26] Lacan will also pay his tribute to
structural relationships (and, thereby, "science") as his first move.
Indeed, he will insist that only Saussure's linguistics (unfortunately not available to Freud) can render scientific the discovery of
the unconscious—an unconscious, of course, structured like a
language. Every apophatic mystic in the monotheistic prophetic
traditions will answer their critics in much the same way. Unfortunately, the prophets who wrote our sacred texts did not have
available to them a grammar of the structural relationships of
God-world-soul; fortunately, this grammar is now available to
interpret the text correctly.

If the grammatical-structuralist move is the only move that the
mystic makes, then all may be well: as the love-mystics hoped, as
religious metaphysicians like Aquinas insist, as the Jungians with
their strangely morphological if not structuralist archetypes
believe, as all structuralists, from Saussure to Levi-Strauss, find
sufficient.

---

[26] On Eckhart, see transl. and intro. Edmund College, O.S.A. and Bernard
McGinn, *Meister Eckhart: The Essential Sermons, Commentaries, Treatises, and
Defense* (New York: Paulist, 1981). John Caputo, *Heidegger and Aquinas: An
Essay in Overcoming Metaphysics* (New York: Fordham University Press, 1982).

But what if a second move is made? What if the apophatic element in mystical discourse takes a radical turn? Then, as in pseudo-Dionysus, Eriugena and Eckhart, the basic structural elements themselves (God-world-soul) dissolve into one another as self-negating, self-dissolving. When Eckhart paradoxically prays, "I pray to God to save me from God," he is not speaking classical prophetic rhetoric of humble submission to the will of God. He is rather apophatically moving. But where? Perhaps, after all, into a radical mystical rhetoric of the Other, the "Godhead beyond" the prophets' God? When Eckhart proclaims a vision of *Leben ohne Warum* as a model for the self which is no-self he is far, indeed, from the responsible self of the prophets as well as far from the agapic-erotic self of the Christian love-mystics. When Lacan informs us that "the unconscious is structured like a language" only then to insist that there is no unitary sign since the signifiers and not the signifieds rule (S/s), we are far, indeed, from the "sign" of Saussure and the god *Logos* of the scientific side of Freud. We are somewhere else. Perhaps in the discourse of the Other? Perhaps in the apophatic excess of *jouissance*? Surely not in the ego.

Like Eckhart with his strange appeals to the more orthodox analogical rhetoric for God-language of his fellow Dominican, Thomas Aquinas, Lacan will also occasionally appeal to more orthodox views of the Other. Hence Lacan will appeal to the dialectical rhetoric of the Other in that strangest of orthodox Lutherans, Hegel, and the rhetorical poetics on "Language Speaks" in that oddest of post-Catholic Catholics, Heidegger.[27] In Lacan's rhetoric there speaks, it seems, not only the Unconscious but the Other of the two most significant Greek-Christians of modernity, the Protestant Hegel and the Catholic Heidegger. Both of them, after all, often read as gnomically as Eckhart (whom, not surprisingly, they both respected). Both of them also

---

[27] On Lacan's relationships to Hegel and Heidegger, see the representative studies of Richardson, Casey and Woody, ver Ecke, Green and Vergote in Joseph H. Smith and William Kerrigan, eds., *Interpreting Lacan* (New Haven: Yale University Press, 1983), pp. 49-223.

wanted an end to "theism" and "atheism" alike in favor of an Other who is finally allowed to speak. The orthodox psychoanalytic institutions may expel Lacan as firmly as the papal commission at Avignon condemned certain propositions of Eckhart. Yet both would continue to insist on their higher orthodoxy. For them, only the mystic understands what the prophet really meant for only the mystic knows both the basic structure of the whole and its radically de-structuring actuality.

But even the mystic may eventually find it necessary to adopt a prophetic rhetoric and proclaim the word of the Other. Otherwise, the others in their secure institutions will trivialize and reify the words of the Other once again. If necessary, prophetic actions may follow: leave the official institution, open a new one, close it, and start again is an all too familiar prophetic activity. The careers of Eckhart and Lacan are often as uncannily parallel as their apophatic rhetorics. Neither was interested in either "theism" or "atheism." That quarrel they left to those who did not understand the Other at all. They wanted *jouissance* and the uncanny tropes familiar in the authentic speech of the Other.

The question, "Does Lacan interpret Freud correctly?", therefore, bears remarkable resemblance to the question, "Does the apophatic mystic interpret the prophetic texts correctly?" Despite the decrees of Avignon, the case of Eckhart is still open; so is the case of Lacan. If the prophetic rhetoric needing interpretation is itself, often despite itself, also a speech of the other, it also becomes mystical rhetoric. Then the chances are reasonably good that a mystical interpretation may take hold. And if the mystic, however reluctantly, is forced into a prophetic role, the chances are even better. But neither the theist nor the atheist, neither the scientistic scientist nor the Romantic mythologist (Jung?) need enter this debate. The debate between the prophet and the mystic is elsewhere. It is beside itself. It is a rhetoric of the Other.

THE QUESTION OF CRITERIA
FOR INTER-RELIGIOUS DIALOGUE:
ON REVISITING WILLIAM JAMES

Introduction

As any theologian involved in serious inter-religious dialogue soon learns, her or his earlier theological thoughts on the "other religions" soon become spent. There is no more difficult or more pressing question on the present theological horizon than that of inter-religious dialogue. Part of that question must be the question of possible criteria for the dialogue itself. Such criteria, if available, must not claim to replace the dialogue but, at best, heuristically to inform it.

My own risk in this chapter is to attempt to formulate some general criteria. I am painfully aware of their inadequacy but just as painfully aware of the need to attempt them. In my own case, this interest in inter-religious dialogue arises from three sources: first, the development of modern Western hermeneutics modelled on dialogue and conversation and the pressing question of the applicability or non-applicability of Western hermeneutics to the questions of cross-cultural dialogue and inter-religious dialogue;[1] second, my own involvement for some years in Jewish-Christian

---

[1] For helpful recent and quite different studies of these issues of hermeneutical dialogue and comparison, see Rüdiger Bubner, *Essays in Hermeneutics and Critical Theory* (New York: Columbia University Press, 1988); Robin W. Lovin and Frank E. Reynolds, eds., *Cosmogony and the Ethical Order: New Studies in Comparative Ethics* (Chicago: University of Chicago Press, 1985); Diane P. Michelfelder and Richard E. Palmer, *Dialogue and Deconstruction: The Gadamer-Derrida Encounter* (Albany: State University of New York Press, 1989); Donald K. Swearer, *Dialogue: The Key to Understanding Other Religions* (Philadelphia: Westminster, 1977); Tullis Maranhao, *The Interpretation of Dialogue* (Chicago: University of Chicago Press, 1990); Gayle L. Ormiston and Alan D. Schrift, *The Hermeneutic Tradition: From Ast to Ricoeur* (Albany: State University of New York Press, 1990); Frank Whaling, ed., *The World's Religious Traditions: Essays in Honor of Wilfred Cantwell Smith* (New York: Crossroad, 1986).

dialogues and Buddhist-Christian dialogues as well as in ancient Greek religion; third, the impact for me of the work of Mircea Eliade and the challenge of his great retrieval of the archaic religions for all theological thought and the impact of the daring and ground-breaking work of my colleague, Langdon Gilkey, with his categories of "parity" and "relative absolutes."[2]

My strategy—a groping one, I admit—is as follows: to return to a thinker who tried honestly to face this question in early modernity, William James, in order to see what revisions may be needed in the general criteria he once advanced. Accordingly, the present essay has two parts: first, an interpretation of James' own position and then a reformulation of his criteria for contemporary discussions. Hence, I shall try to formulate the kind of criteria that may prove helpful for inter-religious dialogue. If these criteria fail, that too can be a gain: to learn one road not to travel can sometimes be as fruitful as learning the right one.

On Revisiting William James

Why the sudden new interest across the intellectual disciplines in William James? There is, of course, no one answer to this question. But that is already one clue to the elusive character of James' thought and person. More than any other thinker of his period in the early twentieth century James was interested in one of the major questions for almost all late-twentieth century thinkers: the question of pluralism and how it affects all of our reflections on our own tradition and on the impact of other traditions on ourselves. James was catholic in his interests. He loved diversity almost for its own sake—perhaps for the sake of its fidelity to the "buzzing, blooming confusion" of experience itself. He loved learning how others experience the world in the belief that by learning from others we might enrich our own tradition and finally understand its uniqueness. He distrusted totalizing systems of all sorts. He refused to believe that the world

---

[2] See Langdon Gilkey's essay in John Hick and Paul Knitter, eds., *The Myth of Christian Uniqueness* (New York: Orbis, 1987).

in all its plurality could ever be reduced to only one monistic formula.[3] He loved thought that was directed to action, to articulating and putting into practice new possibilities.[4]

In psychology, for example, James is often said to be pre-Freudian. And so he was. There is little of Freud's profoundly tragic vision of how our past traps us in James and there is even less of Freud's classic emphasis on sexuality. And yet, in another sense, Freud and most post-Freudians can be called pre-Jamesian: for there is little of James' future-orientation, his daring attempt to try ever new possibilities for action and future transformation in the archeological orientation toward the past of classic psychoanalysis. James was more generous with others than with himself and precisely this generosity of spirit and vision led to occasional confusion and even internal contradictions in his thought and practice. Keen psychologist that he was, James knew that we are all the victims of both our vices and our virtues. His characteristic virtue of generosity to the opinions of others occasionally became a vice. But, for James, this kind of difficulty was preferable to the more common vice of refusing to hear any voice other than one's own. James' generosity, moreover, had a nice fighting edge to it. Life itself, he insisted, does not feel like something that merely happens to us. Life feels like a fight, James insisted—so why not be the Happy Warrior willing to listen to all, struggle with and for all, help all to hear other voices than the self? It was probably that "happy warrior" side of James that led his former student, Santayana, to call him "this Irishman let loose among the Brahmins of Harvard!"[5]

There are two aspects of James' thought and spirit which, as I shall emphasize in the body of this chapter, render his thought particularly attractive to thinkers concerned with the inter-reli-

[3] William James, *A Pluralistic Universe* (Cambridge: Harvard University Press, 1979).

[4] See, especially, William James, *Pragmatism* (Cambridge: Harvard University Press, 1976); and William James, *The Meaning of Truth: A Sequel to Pragmatism* (Cambridge: Harvard University Press, 1977).

[5] See the introductory essay by Andrew M. Greeley in William James, *The Varieties of Religious Experience* (Garden City: Doubleday, 1978), pp. 1-20.

gious dialogue. The first might be called the Jamesian instinct for plurality united to a sense that there is also a unity-amidst-the-diversity of life. James' typical intellectual strategy, like that of the best of classical Catholic philosophy and theology, was to honor diversity while seeking analogies amid the diversity itself. Differences need not become dialectical oppositions[6] but can become analogies, that is, similarities-in-difference. This classic strategy of Catholic thought—what I have elsewhere called its analogical imagination—was also fully characteristic of William James. Such an analogical imagination, at its best, can affirm the remarkable unity-in-diversity of reality without reducing all reality to "more of the same." This analogical imagination also led James to posit two religious "intense cases" that might disclose the ultimate mystery to us: those James named the "mystics" and the "saints."[7] Protestant thought of James' period was not, on the whole, eager to reflect theologically on the realities of the "saint" and the "mystic." James, characteristically, was. For James believed, as do I, that reflection even by non-mystics and non-saints on what he nicely named these "extreme cases" of human possibility may be our best clues to the mystery of religion. If you want to understand what most of us are like most of the time, then do not choose the "mystics" and the "saints" for your analysis. But if you want to understand what human beings can be when they break out of self-centeredness into Reality-centeredness, then reflect, with James, not just on yourself but on the two extreme types: the cognitive extremity of the mystic and the action-transforming extremity of the saint.

The most notable fact about William James on religion is the sheer multiplicity of his responses and interests. There is no one

---

[6] It is significant here to note how several post-modern French thinkers insist on the category "difference" against the dialectical category of "otherness." For example, contrast Gilles Deleuze, *Différence et répetition* (Paris: Presses Universitaires de France, 1968), and Michael Theunissen, *The Other: Studies in the Ontology of Husserl, Heidegger, Sartre and Buber* (Cambridge: MIT Press, 1984).

[7] On "saints," see James, *Varieties of Religious Experience*, pp. 261-370; on "mystics," pp. 370-418.

Jamesian way either to describe or to assess "religion." Unlike Kant, there is no single Jamesian argument on religion. James' position is less like an argument and more like a rather diverse and sometimes rambling conversation. It is a conversation filled with valuable and sometimes extraordinary insights on how to describe religion in all its variety and how to assess it in all its complexity.

James' own final position on religion he named (in the *Varieties of Religious Experience*) a "piecemeal" supernaturalism.[8] My own interpretation of his position here might be named a "piecemeal" interpretation—and that for largely the same reasons that he resisted a "wholesale" supernaturalism. The latter seems improbable. The former seems both possible and promising. I shall, therefore, signal a few typically Jamesian moves on religion—or at least those which seem most characteristically James and most worth discussing.

James distinguishes himself from most Western philosophers of religion by his insistence on variety. To read his classic work *The Varieties of Religion* is to be exposed to a remarkable range of religious options: from classics like Wesley and Teresa of Avila or Luther and Al-Ghazzali to a whole range of then contemporary memoirs collected by Starburck and others. An insistence on how various religion is—to the point where it may be difficult even to use the word "religion"—has become something of a commonplace among several scholars in contemporary religious studies (e.g., W.C. Smith and John Cobb).[9] James felt at home in the word "religion" and even in defining its common characteristics (even if he does that in different ways in *The Varieties* alone!). James also believed that in all that difference there was enough commonality to allow us to speak coherently of "religion" prima-

---

[8] Ibid., pp. 500-507.

[9] Wilfred Cantwell Smith, *The Meaning and End of Religion: A New Approach to the Religious Traditions of Mankind* (New York: Macmillan, 1963); John B. Cobb, Jr., "The Religions" in Peter C. Hodgson and Robert H. King, eds., *Christian Theology: An Introduction to Its Traditions and Tasks* (Philadelphia: Fortress, 1982), pp. 299-323.

rily as "the feelings, acts, and experiences of individual men in their solitude, so far as they apprehend themselves to stand in relation to whatever they may consider the divine."[10]

But even granted (for James) these commonalities (now controverted), it is clear that it is the sheer variety—the "republican feast" side—of religion which attracted James most. There is truth to the various charges that James' own "variety" was highly limited. For James' choices, however various, were also very late Victorian: many selections from Christianity, some from Judaism and Islam, some comments on the other "high" religions (Buddhism, Hinduism) with most other religions thrown together as "pagan" (the Greek and Roman religions) or "savage" (the primal or archaic religions). At the same time one must note James' clear interest in and commitment to the then nascent "science of religions."[11] James believed that this new discipline (far more than theology or philosophy) was the primary hope both for describing religions *and* for assessing them.

What consistently interested James in the religions was religious experience, especially the "feeling" element. What interested him was what he named a "full fact"[12]: "a conscious field *plus* its object as felt or thought of *plus* an attitude towards the object *plus* the sense of a self to whom the attitude belongs." The best of James on religion, I believe, is in his insistence on personal experience as the primary locus for religion and as that which needs both describing and assessing. Of course, this Jamesian position does exact a price—namely a failure to account for other crucial aspects of the religious phenomenon, such as the institutional or even social (recall von Hugel or Royce or Troeltsch among James' own contemporaries) or the more strictly intellectual expressions in philosophies and theologies (recall the Hege-

[10] On this side of James' enterprise, see Henry Samuel Levinson, *The Religious Investigations of William James* (Chapel Hill: University of North Carolina Press, 1981).

[11] *Varieties of Religious Experience*, p. 49.

[12] Ibid., p. 393. On "full fact" in James, see John Wild, *The Radical Empiricism of William James* (Garden City: Doubleday, 1969).

lians and neo-Kantians among James' contemporaries). It is odd, I admit, that the great proponent of the variety of religious experiences neglected such crucial aspects of religion as the institutional and the intellectual.

Odd, but not fatal: for James clearly knew that here he was partial—but partial for a reason. The reason remains worth dwelling upon. Many philosophers and theologians seem finally not very interested in what religious persons may experience (or think they experience). Rather they are interested only in whatever cognitive claims religious experience entails. Many philosophers seem interested only in the cognitive beliefs implied or entailed by religious faith rather than trying to describe and assess the experience which faith as a fundamental orientation involves. It is not that James was not interested in the assessment of the cognitive claims: as we shall see below, he was very interested—and, I think, very interesting. It is, rather, that James believed that most philosophical and theological attempts at assessing religion analyze only the "cognitive claim" (or "belief") side of religious experience—and fail to recognize that this is a limitation. Then "religion," as analyzed by many philosophers and theologians, can become a phenomenon that involves some rather strange, not to say odd or bizarre, "beliefs" that demand cognitive assessment. At its clearest, this position becomes a "religion is really x" position. Recall Santayana for whom "religion is poetry which intervenes in life; poetry is religion which supervenes upon life." Recall Braithwaite for whom religion is really morality with some stories added to help one internalize the morality. Recall W.C. Clifford (James' adversary in *The Will To Believe*) for whom religion seems to be an immoral credulousness in odd and unpersuasive cognitive claims or beliefs.

For William James, religion, above all, is some kind of personal experience: at its best a "full fact" experience. Because religion as experience must first be described before any assessment, James turned to classic documents which purported to describe religious experience. Because religious experience needs to be described in its distinctive characteristics *as* religious (rather than by means of those characteristics it shares with morality, art, metaphysics, etc.), James next appealed to the "extreme cases" (e.g. the "saints" and the "mystics"). James was not interested in the "extreme cases" only because of their extremity. Indeed, if that were so, why did he provide so generous an account of the "healthy-minded?"[13] Why not only the "extreme cases" of the "healthy-minded" (like Walt Whitman or Emerson) rather than such less extreme versions as the "mind-cure" movements or "liberal Christianity?" Those interested in extreme cases, moreover, are usually interested principally, if not exclusively, in "sick-soul" types.

Any analyst of religious experience should, I believe, at some point follow James' advice and study *first* (not *only*) the "extreme cases" in all their variety—from "sick-soul" to "healthy-minded," from James' mystic and saint, to Eliade's shaman and guru, to Buber's prophet. In one sense, James' strategy follows a suggestion often voiced: "I may not be able to define religion but I know it when I see it." Whatever *else* Wesley or Luther or Teresa of Avila or John of the Cross are, they are recognizably religious. If we can, in some descriptive manner, analyze their experience by interpreting their texts, we will find good candidates for characteristics which may prove recognizably religious.

The logic of James' move from analyzing "personal experience" by interpreting "extreme case" documents remains a plausible strategy for anyone wishing to describe one crucial aspect of religion: namely, the individual's experience of religion insofar as others can understand that experience by interpreting it. Such descriptions, if successful, would admittedly not cover the institutional and the strictly intellectual aspects of religion. Nevertheless such descriptions would cover, for James, the heart of the matter: those experiences which are distinctively religious. Most of the *Varieties* is concerned with description of such personal experiences—the latter, to repeat, as interpreted through various documents.

[13] James, *Varieties of Religious Experience*, pp. 92-138.

James' ways of assessing or evaluating religious experience were, moreover, as various as his descriptions of religious experience itself. I make no claim to interpret all his many strategies of assessment, and they were *many* from the *Principles of Psychology* through the *Pragmatism* essays to *A Pluralistic Universe* to the final—or was it?—position of *Essays in Radical Empiricism*. My own belief is that to render James' position of assessing or evaluating any phenomenon, especially religion, strictly coherent would not do justice to the "buzzing, blooming confusion" of the experience that William James was intent on communicating with all his rhetorical skill.

Nevertheless there are still some modes of evaluation which are characteristically Jamesian, both early and late. First consider James' essays on assessing religious belief personally for oneself—his psychological and philosophical assessments of religious belief. The most famous of such studies are, to be sure, those in the *Essays in Morality and Religion*, especially the famous *The Will to Believe* essay.[14] As James later recognized, this essay (and the larger project in the other related essays) might have been more helpfully named "The Right to Believe." By his haste (and perhaps his wish to provoke) James handed his critics an easy charge: that he was defending sheer "fideism" with his "will to believe." Indeed, the furor over the "will to believe" phrase was analogous to the clamor over his equally unfortunate phrase: the "cash-value" of an idea.

What James really attempted to defend with "religious belief," however, was the "right to believe." In general, for James, we have such a right whenever the beliefs in question are "live," "forced" and "momentous." By a "live" hypothesis James meant a real possibility which could guide one's conduct. If a belief could not guide a person's conduct, then a decision for or against that belief is no decision at all: it is dead.

Decisions are "forced" only if, besides being "live" options,

---

[14] William James, *The Will to Believe and Other Essays* (Cambridge: Harvard University Press, 1982).

they also possess the characteristic that there is no possibility of not choosing one of two logically distinct options presented. Such "live and forced" options present the imperative "either accept this truth or go without it."

"Momentous," as distinct from trivial, decisions are characterized by their ability to disclose a major difference for life. For James, authentic decisions on all beliefs, including religious beliefs, should be live, forced, and momentous. Note how for James "live" options tended towards criteria of conduct; "forced" options to criteria of logical coherence, and "momentous" options to criteria of personal experience.[15]

There is, moreover, "rough coherence" between James' position on evaluating religious belief "from within" in his *Will To Believe* essay and his assessment of religious experience from "outside" the analogous criteria developed in the sometimes disparate comments on criteria of assessment in the *Varieties* itself. Indeed, this rough coherence was present in James all along or, as he liked to say, "on the whole." On the whole, I read James (who once quipped that his position should be named "on the wholeism") as holding to the same *kind* of criteria whether judging non-religious phenomena (as in the *Principles* or in the *Pragmatism* essays) or religious phenomena (either from "within" as in the *Will To Believe*, or from "outside" as in the *Varieties*).

These general criteria are:

In psychological terms (best expressed in *The Principles of Psychology*), one can find an adequate psychological description of a given reality only when one can account for perceptions (including experience in the broad sense—i.e., feelings, moods, attitudes not only "sense-experience" as in classical empiricism), conceptions, and volitions.

In philosophical terms (which are, for James, largely terms of assessment just as psychological terms are largely terms of description), one needs criteria of a full empiricism—indeed, finally, a radical empiricism where the Jamesian revisionary notion of

[15] Ibid., pp. 13-33.

experience is given full sway. For James "experience" is not limited to sense experience (as in British empiricism) but includes feelings, mood, and what Whitehead (here influenced by James) named non-sensuous perception. This "wider" Jamesian notion of experience allows the American empirical tradition to appeal to experiences of relationships; the relation of self with itself, others, and with the whole. One also needs criteria of logical coherence: James' weakest link, as critics from Royce to Russell, and even frustrated allies like Peirce, insisted. Finally, one needs pragmatic criteria to assess the ethical consequences for action of all our ideas and experiences.

Psychologically and philosophically these roughly coherent Jamesian criteria for both description and evaluation of any phenomenon are also the criteria present in James' actual descriptions and evaluations of religious experience in the *Varieties*. In brief, note the rough coherence of the psychological and philosophical criteria cited above with James' insistence in the *Varieties* that "on the whole" the criteria for assessment of religious experience are:[16]

(1) "immediate luminousness" (i.e., perception and personal experience in the broad, even radical sense noted above);

(2) coherence with what we otherwise know or believe to be the case (as in the description of live, forced, momentous options);

(3) individual and social practical consequences (pragmatic criteria).

If my interpretation of James is plausible on this controverted issue, then it may also partly illuminate three puzzles in James. First, James' concern with mysticism is a concern, above all, to try to describe and assess any claims to "immediate luminousness" for mystics and what this might mean for non-mystics when they are observing mystics. Second, James' concern with "saintliness" is principally a concern with consequences—and interestingly enough, for so famous an individualist, principally for the *social* consequences of the "saint."

[16] James, *Varieties of Religious Experience*, p. 37.

Third, the whole of the assessment of religion in the *Varieties* must cohere with what one otherwise knows and believes (e.g., in psychology and philosophy). This is why, I believe, James held that mystics would find their experience irrefutable but the rest of us could not accord it that status. We could, however, affirm that the mystics' accounts of their experience do allow us non-mystics to state our belief (which coheres with but is clearly not identical with theirs) in the reality of "something more."

In sum, James remains intriguing because he seems so basically fair to the variety of religious experiences he describes and so subtle and coherent in his tentative assessments of these experiences. On the whole, William James *is* a good interpreter and assessor of the variety of religious experiences for he is often immediately luminous in what he says, he is roughly coherent in the ways suggested above and he does also develop useful pragmatic modes of assessment for ethical consequences. William James remains the classic early modern student of religious pluralism.

A Rethinking of Jamesian Criteria:
Possibility, Coherence, Ethical Consequences

However suggestive James' classic study of the variety of religious experience may be, it is equally important to emphasize its severe limitations. Much has happened since James—in philosophy, in theology, in history of religions and, above all, in history itself. His candidates for religious pluralism, however generous for the early twentieth century, seem now clearly limited, Western, even parochial. It is not merely the relative lack of attention James accords the great traditions of Asia—especially Buddhism in all its plurality and Hinduism with its traditions of pluralism. It is the fact that these great traditions have now also become genuine "live" options for Westerners. Western Buddhists—especially in the United States—have changed traditional Asian forms of Buddhism in notable ways: recall Jeffrey Hopkins, Robert Thurman, and the thinkers of Naropa Institute in

Tibetan Buddhism; or Francis Cook and others in Zen Buddhism. Recall as well the fruitfulness of the many Buddhist-Christian dialogues.[17] The Western Buddhists have not merely rendered Buddhism a live option for many Westerners but have subtly changed Buddhism itself as radically as the earlier classic shifts from India to Thailand, Tibet, China and Japan once did.[18] The power and attractiveness of many gurus and Hindu mythologies and philosophical thought among Westerners has also yielded yet new Western forms of Hinduism and Sikhism for Westerners.

Moreover, the magisterial work of Mircea Eliade on the great archaic and primal traditions as well as the explosion of work by historians of religions and anthropologists on many religious locative traditions in Oceania, Africa, and the Americas has exponentially increased the radical variety of religion beyond James' imagination.[19] In Christian theology alone, the number of theologians who now acknowledge that Christian self-understanding can no longer treat the question of religious pluralism in either traditional exclusivist or even classical inclusivist categories has increased greatly: from the pioneering work and often conflicting proposals of Raimondo Pannikar, W.C. Smith, John Hick and John Cobb to the recent work of Julia Ching, Langdon Gilkey, Paul Knitter, Gordon Kaufman, Leonard Swidler, Rosemary Ruether, Will Oxtoby, Schubert Ogden, Hans Küng, Wolfhart Pannenberg and many others. The list of strictly theological proposals for serious inter-religious dialogue is now at the point where it is difficult to understand how any serious theologian in any tradition would not admit the challenge to ordinary theology of the issue of religious pluralism. The expanding list of "live

[17] See the journal *Buddhist-Christian Studies* for representative texts.

[18] See H. Beckert and R. Gombrich, eds., *The World of Buddhism* (London: Thames & Hudson, 1984); Henri Dumoulin, ed., *Buddhism in the Modern World* (New York: Collier, 1976); William Peiris, *The Western Contribution to Buddhism* (New Delhi: Motilal Banarsidass, 1973).

[19] For a representative work here, see Lawrence E. Sullivan, *Icanchu's Drum: An Orientation to Meaning in South American Religions* (New York: Macmillan, 1988).

options" and conflicting proposals either for dialogue or resulting from dialogue make contemporary theology more and more genuinely pluralistic amidst a conflict of interpretations.

On the philosophical side, moreover, James' relatively sanguine contentment with the categories "experience" and "religious experience" has now been properly (and, I have argued elsewhere, correctly) challenged by the linguistic turn in all its permutations and conflicts.[20] Those conflicts include the recent centrality given to radical plurality in post-structuralist thought (centered around the category "difference") and the increasing sense of the ambiguity of all traditions exposed by history itself and by the many new forms of ideology-critique and dialectical thought (centered around the category "the other"). Even the category "religion," as is well known, has come under increasing suspicion for its Western (more exactly Romano-Christian) overtones.

In such an intellectually parlous situation it may seem an odd choice to return to one of the earliest modern attempts to deal intellectually with religious pluralism, William James. My apologies for my choice must be a brief one. James' *Varieties of Religious Experience* is, I continue to believe, a classic. Like all classics, it combines a curious datedness with an excess and permanence of meaning which yield fruitful reflection for later interpreters. Such, at least, is my belief on classics in general and on the *Varieties of Religious Experience* in particular. I will now risk that belief by trying to show how James' very general, flexible, and fruitful criteria might be reformulated for our present concern for some generic criteria for serious inter-religious dialogue.

James' category of "immediate luminousness" can be usefully shifted to the basic hermeneutical category of "suggestive possibility."[21] Insofar as hermeneutics since Gadamer is grounded in the

---

[20] See David Tracy, *Plurality and Ambiguity: Hermeneutics, Religion and Hope* (San Francisco: Harper & Row, 1987), pp. 47-66.

[21] Martin Heidegger, "The Origin of the Work of Art" and "Building, Dwelling, Thinking," in David Krell, ed., *Basic Writings* (New York: Harper & Row, 1977); see also David Halliburton, *Poetic Thinking: An Approach to Heidegger* (Chicago: University of Chicago Press, 1981); James J. Di Censo,

category of conversation and dialogue, and insofar as hermeneutics is fashioned to relate experience directly to language, hermeneutics proves a fruitful philosophical tradition for all concerned with the meaning and import of all serious dialogue and the direct (i.e., through language) character of all the "experiences" available for interpretation. Even James, after all, had to rely on texts to interpret the "religious experiences" he believed he was interpreting.

Moreover, as post-Gadamerian hermeneutics has yielded its own history-of-effects, there is now available, pace Gadamer, a greater role both for explanatory methods (Ricoeur), ideology-critique (Habermas) and plurality than an earlier hermeneutics envisaged. A notion of "dialogue" which has no place for these central intellectual, moral, and even religious demands is one tempted, alas, by too easy notions of "similarity" or even "sameness," and too sanguine a notion of the complementarity of all the religions.

Granted these important caveats, hermeneutics shows how dialogue remains the central hope for recognizing the "possibilities" (and, therefore, the live options) which any serious conversation with the "other" and the "different" can yield. It matters relatively little whether the dialogue is through person-to-person dialogue or through that peculiar form of dialogue we call serious reading of texts, rituals, or events. To recognize the other *as* other, the different *as* different is also to acknowledge that other world of meaning as, in some manner, a possible option for myself. The traditional language of analogy may still prove, in admittedly a new form, one way to formulate how, after any genuine dialogue, what once seemed merely other now seems a

Hermeneutics and the Disclosure of Truth: A Study in the Work of Heidegger, Gadamer and Ricoeur (Charlottesville: University Press of Virginia, 1990); Daniel Guerrière, ed., *Phenomenology of the Truth Proper to Religion* (Albany: State University of New York Press, 1990). Note also the relevant works cited in note 1. For Gadamer, see, especially, Hans-Georg Gadamer, *Truth and Method* (New York: Seabury, 1975), especially pp. 91-119, 235-354. For my own reflections on the hermeneutic tradition, see *Plurality and Ambiguity*, pp. 1-47.

real possibility and thereby, in some manner, similar to what I have already experienced (including religiously). I acknowledge that I and others who are trying to formulate "an analogical imagination" as one strategy for envisioning religious pluralism must be not only wary but downright suspicious of how easily claims to "analogy" or "similarity" can become subtle evasions of the other and the different. Similarity cannot be a cover-word for the rule of the same. Hence we still need to remind ourselves linguistically of this great danger by speaking not of "analogies" simply as "similarities" but of analogies as always similarities-in-difference.[22]

But whatever the fate of the strategy of "an analogical imagination" for rendering the possibilities discovered through dialogue into similarities-in-difference, the larger issue is elsewhere: namely, in the category of "possibility" itself. My earlier shift from James' category of "immediate luminousness" to the category of "suggestive possibility" means that the adjective "suggestive" can serve as a reminder that "possibility" need not be a "live, momentous and forced" option for the interpreter in order to prove a genuine possibility. As reception-theory (Jauss) in hermeneutics reminds us, a whole spectrum of responses to any classic is available. That spectrum can range all the way from a shock of recognition (in aesthetic terms) or "faith" or "enlightenment" (in religious terms) to a sense of tentative resonance to a genuine, that is, live, but not forced or momentous, option, on the other end of the spectrum. The spectrum remains a real spectrum (and not mere congeries of responses) insofar as any genuine *possibility* evoked by the conversation itself is produced. What little I understand of Buddhist "compassion" I do not understand on inner-Buddhist grounds of enlightenment. Yet I can respond and have responded to that classic notion with a resonance to the challenge it poses to my own Christian notions of love.

[22] For this category and its relationship to hermeneutics, see David Tracy, *The Analogical Imagination: Christian Theology and the Culture of Pluralism* (New York: Crossroad, 1981), pp. 91-154, 405-57.

1st criteria, based on James

A further advantage of the hermeneutical category of suggestive possibility produced by serious inter-religious dialogue is the fundamentally aesthetic rather than ethical character of the category "possibility." The hermeneutical tradition from Heidegger through Gadamer and Ricoeur has defended the primordial notion of truth-as-manifestation (not correspondence, strict coherence, or empirical verification or falsification). This notion of truth as manifestation (more exactly, with Heidegger, as disclosure-concealment) has two singular advantages for this first general set of criteria for inter-religious dialogue. The first advantage is that the notion of truth-as-manifestation more closely fits both notions of "revelation" or its analogues in many religions and notions of "enlightenment" in other religions or ways. The same notion of religious manifestation, like the experience of truth in works of art, also frees this first set of criteria to have a more aesthetic rather than either ethical or "scientific" cast. The advantage here (as James with his category of "immediate luminousness" and his focus on the "mystics" for "cognitive" issues also implicitly recognized) is that the question of criteria for truth in religious dialogue will not only be ethical-pragmatic or scientific-metaphysical. Although the latter criteria remain relevant, as we shall see below, the imposition (especially by Western partners to the interreligious dialogue) of solely ethical (e.g., justice or social-political liberation) or solely verificationist or Western metaphysical criteria would be challenged.

The truth of religion is, like the truth of its nearest cousin, art, primordially the truth of manifestation.[23] Hermeneutical thought, with its defense of this notion, is well-suited to defend anew this primal insight of both art and religion. In that sense, hermeneutics (with its attendant criteria) is useful for reopening the highly complex questions of mysticism, revelation, and enlightenment. Hermeneutics may also help to reopen the question of

---

[23] See references in note 20. In Christian theology, see John Riches, ed., *The Analogy of Beauty: The Theology of Hans Urs von Balthasar* (Edinburgh: T. & T. Clark, 1986).

why so many Buddhist thinkers (especially Zen) refuse too sharp a distinction between the aesthetic and the religious.

As further developments within Western hermeneutics indicate, however, one need not and should not stop in the dialogue with that first set of criteria anymore than James stopped with "immediate luminousness." One should, nonetheless, dwell there long enough to allow the truth of the other to become, somewhere along the spectrum, a genuine possibility for oneself, in however transformed a form. To understand at all is to understand differently. To understand at all is to understand for and within genuine dialogue allowing real manifestations of the other's truth and thereby mutual transformation. The kind of further questions appropriate for the dialogue and thereby the kind of further general criteria available can now be clarified by a return to and reformulation of James' other two sets of criteria.

Let us name the second set of criteria a rough coherence with what we otherwise know or more likely believe to be the case. The danger here is that, especially for Western conversation-partners, this set of cognitive criteria (under rubrics, for example, like strict verification and strict falsification) will so quickly take over that the notion of truth in art and religion as manifestatory will become a distant memory.

Here, surely, several recent Western philosophical discussions of reason itself are helpful for fighting that scientistic (not scientific) temptation.[24] In an intellectual situation where even philosophers of natural science (e.g., Toulmin) have challenged earlier reigning paradigms of scientism and "rationality," many (to be

[24] See Richard J. Bernstein, *Beyond Objectivism and Relativism: Science, Hermeneutics and Praxis* (Philadelphia: University of Pennsylvania Press, 1983); Richard J. Bernstein, *The Restructuring of Social and Political Theory* (New York: Harcourt, Brace, Jovanovich, 1976); John Rajchaan and Cornel West, eds., *Post-Analytic Philosophy* (New York: Columbia University Press, 1985); Stephen Toulmin, *Human Understanding*. Vol. 1. *The Collective Use and Evolution of Concepts.* (Princeton: Princeton University Press, 1972); Kenneth Baynes, James Bohnian and Thomas McCarthy, eds., *After Philosophy: End or Transformation?* (Cambridge: MIT Press, 1987); Fred R. Dallmayr, *Critical Encounters Between Philosophy and Politics* (Notre Dame: University of Notre Dame Press, 1987).

sure, not all) in the philosophical community have far more flexible notions of "truth" and "reason" than was the case in the heyday of positivism. Science itself is now acknowledged as a hermeneutic enterprise. What one now finds is a historically and hermeneutically informed philosophy of science (Toulmin) as well as a philosophically informed history of science. It is not only the case, as Hegel insisted, that the fact that reason has a history is a problem for reason. It is also the case that the history of reason includes the history of relatively adequate (e.g., Aristotle) and inadequate (e.g., positivism) accounts of reason. Hence the emergence of historically informed theories of rationality (Apel-Habermas-Bernstein). I do not pretend by these brief references to imply that the problem of an adequate notion of reason is readily available. Of course, there is no *de facto* consensus among contemporary philosophers on what rational consensus in principle is. This, for the purposes of the interreligious dialogue, is not necessarily unfortunate. If philosophers like Bernstein show a genuinely rational way to recover the classical resources of reason (e.g., Aristotelian *phronesis* and Peirce's community of inquiry') then, minimally, the discussion of "reason and religion" should be freed from what Bernstein nicely labels both "objectivism" and "relativism."[25] Those two options—so familiar in the recent past and so fatal for serious dialogue of any sort—are spent. Rather we are left with more flexible but no less rational criteria for the rough coherence of what truths-as-manifestations we may glean from art and religion with what we otherwise know from science or, more likely, with what we believe in accordance with the present consensus of rational inquirers.

The situation for interreligious dialogue (as for comparative studies in history of religions) has become, in sum, far more flexible. Some believe that the best step forward (in keeping with Aristotelian *phronesis*) is to find concrete examples for dialogue on comparison (e.g., Christian love and Buddhist compassion). We can dialogue on such concrete issues in order to see, by

[25] Bernstein, *Beyond Objectivism and Relativism*.

fidelity to the logic of the questioning set loose by the subject-matter, what ensues. This strategy—which has proved so fruitful in contemporary philosophy of science—is surely one promising step forward. If the demands of reason in concrete cases are observed, if a rough coherence between the truths of religion and art and the truths of science and philosophy does obtain in the dialogue, that can, for the moment, suffice. This *solvitur ambulando* strategy, so congenial to James, can be one proper strategy for the contemporary inter-religious dialogue with the crucial proviso that the demands of reason, including the proper demands of metaphysical and transcendental reflection, must be allowed full sway in every conversation worthy of the name.

As any participant in serious inter-religious dialogue soon discovers, moreover, a further set of criteria will and should emerge—generically, ethical-political criteria. These criteria, so familiar to the prophetic trajectories of the religions, enter the conversation by two routes. First, the religions themselves, especially but not solely in their prophetic strands, demand them. Secondly, our very nature as human beings demands ethical assessment. For example, it is noteworthy how frequently Jewish, Christian, and Islamic conversation partners, in fidelity to both their prophetic heritages and to their contemporary ethical-political concerns, raise these issues in inter-religious dialogues: recall John Hick's recent work,[26] or Hans Küng's criterion of the *humanum*, or Emil Fackenheim's Jewish post-Holocaust "return to history," or Fazlur Rahman's revisionary Islamic theology, or Rosemary Radford Ruether's Christian feminist concerns or Rita Gross' Buddhist feminist concerns or Paul Knitter's liberationist emphasis.

The "pragmatic" turn of hermeneutics itself—as indeed of much contemporary discourse philosophy—fully shares in this insistence on the need for ethical-political criteria. In that sense, we are all heirs of James' insistence on the criteria of "ethical,

[26] See, especially, John Hick, *An Interpretation of Religion: Human Responses to the Transcendent* (New Haven: Yale University Press, 1989).

humane" fruits, or consequences for action—both individually and societally. Even here, however, our situation is more difficult and more parlous than the one James envisaged. On the "individual" side, the rampant problems of individualism (Bellah, *et. al.*) have become a major ethical dilemma for modern Western societies. More pressing still, the very notion of the "self," so cherished in almost all Western philosophies and theologies (even those, like process thought, highly critical of earlier "substantialist" notions of the self), has become a central problem in inter-religious dialogues where several highly sophisticated Buddhist notions of "no-self" enter to radicalize all more familiar Western notions of "self."

The ethical-social-political criteria meet similar challenges: above all from the philosophical discovery of the inevitability of social-political realities of power embedded in all discourse and the Jewish-Christian-and-Islamic reformulations of the prophetic strands of these traditions into several distinct and often competing liberationist theologies.[27] Here James' pragmatic criteria of ethical (and, by implication, social and political) consequences for action (recall his analysis of "saints") provides a useful set of general and flexible criteria for serious inter-religious dialogue.

That these criteria need further reflection and refinement beyond the brief analysis given above (or beyond even my more extended reflections on them elsewhere) is obvious. Even if these criteria are, on the whole, sound, they still cannot replace the actual inter-religious dialogue but only inform it with the appropriate kind of questions as well as some generic and heuristic criteria. However, such criteria may still aid participants as we struggle on the *terra incognita* of a present acknowledgment of religious pluralism as the question for all serious religious thinkers in all traditions. For that *terra incognita* is now our true home.

---

[27] On the prophetic tradition in relationship to liberation theologies, see Roger Haight, *An Alternative Vision: An Interpretation of Liberation Theology* (New York: Paulist, 1985), especially chapter 5.

THE CHALLENGE OF THE ARCHAIC OTHER:
THE HERMENEUTICS OF MIRCEA ELIADE

The Archaic Other and Christian Theology

The challenge of the other to modern Christian theological self-understanding is multifaceted.[1] The inter-religious dialogue has occasioned, for Christian theologians, different dialogical experiences of otherness. Sometimes the initial difficulty is that the dialogue-partner seems so radically other to all our usual modes of thought and practice that dialogue is difficult even to begin and, once begun, to continue with any assurance of fruitful conversation. As we shall see in the next essay, the Buddhist-Christian dialogue can prove of this first type.

At still other times, the problem of the otherness of the other takes a very different form. As in the crucial Jewish-Christian dialogue, the problem can be that the Christian (rarely, since Franz Rosenzweig, the Jew) may be tempted to believe that the dialogue partner is so similar to us as barely to be other at all. This is, I have become convinced after several years in the Jewish-Christian dialogue, a serious Christian mistake. As I have written elsewhere (and I shall not, therefore, repeat here) the problem of the Jewish-Christian dialogue, especially one where the Holocaust is accorded theological weight, is the Christian's need to acknowl-

---

[1] For the philosophical issues, see Michael Theunissen, *The Other: Studies in the Social Ontology of Husserl, Heidegger, Sartre and Buber* (Cambridge, MA: MIT Press, 1984); for selections in theological reflections, *inter alia*, see Wilfred Cantwell Smith, *Towards a World Theology: Faith and the Comparative History of Religions* (Philadelphia: Westminster, 1980); John Hick and Brian Hebblethwaite, eds., *Christianity and Other Religions* (Philadelphia: Fortress, 1980); Peter L. Berger, ed., *The Other Side of God: A Polarity in World Religions* (New York: Doubleday, 1981); Paul Knitter, *No Other Name?* (Maryknoll: Orbis, 1985); Hans Küng, with Josef van Ess, Heinrich von Stietencron, and Heinz Beckert, *Christianity and the World Religions* (New York: Doubleday, 1986).

edge and find ways to undo Christian history.[2] The historical fact is that, from the beginning of the struggle with the synagogue through the centuries of the notorious "teaching of contempt" for the Jew and even today for too many unreflective Christians, the Jew has too often functioned as the "projected other" of the Christian.[3] The terrifying history of Christian anti-Semitism clarifies how Christian self-identity has seemed to involve a notion of the Jew as this projected other. As most Christians now acknowledge with repentance, this notion of the Jew as projected other is surely an unacceptable, indeed a humanly indecent and Christianly irreligious way of achieving Christian self-identity. The Jew and the Christian, along with the Muslim, are profoundly similar, even at times identical in their basic beliefs in God. Nevertheless, they remain profoundly other. Yet this otherness cannot be a projected otherness but only one where the other as other is honored. The Jewish-Christian dialogue and, more truly, the Jewish-Christian-Islamic dialogue, is one of the most important and central facts of our contemporary Christian theological struggle for self-understanding.

At the same time, the problem of the "projected otherness" of the Jew and, to a lesser but real extent, the Muslim in Christian self-consciousness provokes an acknowledgment of another "projected other." All three of the radically monotheistic religions have produced a projected other to their prophetic faith in the God of the covenant: they have named this "other" the "pagans." We forget too easily that "pagan" meant originally the country-folk who held on to the ancient, archaic, and primal traditions. Surely it is time, as many scholars now insist, for theologians to reconsider the archaic traditions. If we are not

[2] For representative essays in this issue, see Elisabeth Schüssler-Fiorenza and David Tracy, eds., *The Holocaust as Event of Interruption, Concilium* 175 (1984), or my Foreword to the important work of Arthur Cohen, *The Tremendum: A Theological Interpretation of the Holocaust* (New York: Crossroad, 1981).

[3] The issue of "otherness" is illuminated by the psychoanalytical category of "projection" here. Too many "dialogues" ignore this "hermeneutics of suspicion" aspect of Christian history in relationship to Judaism in a noble but too sanguine notion of dialogical retrieval.

merely to repeat the tragedies of our history—beginning with the prophetic attacks upon the Canaanites and continuing through the tragedy of what happened to the archaic traditions of Europe and the Americas—surely we must hesitate and we must wonder whether those we name "pagans" may have been forced by our triumphal theologies to be an other invented by our projected fears, desires and needs.

One cannot but hope that the rapid expansion in our day of indigenous African and Melanesian forms of Christianity will not repeat this tragic history of Christianity in Europe and the Americas. As the Christian church becomes a truly world church and not only a Eurocentric one, the relationship of Christian self-understanding to the great archaic or primal traditions becomes a central issue for us all. As historians of religion and as new Christian missiologies throughout the world suggest, there is grave theological need for the contemporary inter-religious dialogue to take seriously these forgotten and, indeed, repressed archaic others. It is difficult but possible to have a serious theological dialogue among representative thinkers of the so-called "higher religions." Yet, as the reality of the archaic traditions remind us all—Jew, Christian, Muslim and Buddhist, Hindu, Sikh and neo-Confucian alike, — the archaic traditions also live with great spiritual power. Moreover, the archaic traditions live embedded, if often repressed, in all the major religious traditions—even the prophetic-oriented religions of the West and the mystically-oriented religions of the East. None of us can continue to ignore the living archaic traditions nor the reality of the archaic in our own tradition. For that reason alone, I believe, the work of Mircea Eliade bears great theological import for Christian theology. As a historian of religion, Eliade devoted his principal attention to the great archaic traditions.[4] As an Eastern Orthodox Christian, Eliade also had the sensibility (so often

---

[4] This is especially true in Eliade's great systematic works: his early *Patterns in Comparative Religion* (London: Sheed and Ward, 1958), as well as his final major work, *A History of Religious Ideas*. 3 Volumes (Chicago: University of Chicago Press, 1978-85).

lacking in Western Catholics and Protestants) for a cosmic Christianity that would not allow its own roots in the archaic to be simply uprooted by a prophetic critique. Eliade produced a new hermeneutics of the archaic other which can help the contemporary Christian theologian and others rethink both hermeneutics and the inter-religious dialogue as a hermeneutics of the other and an inter-religious dialogue where the archaic traditions are taken with full seriousness.

With characteristic modesty, Mircea Eliade claimed that he did not work out a *theory* of hermeneutics, but was guided by what he named a "creative hermeneutics" in all his work. As many scholars have shown, it is indeed Eliade's practice of interpretation which proved so fruitful for all interpretation-theory. Yet, one can, I believe, say more—at least, I shall attempt to do so by some reflections on how Eliade's entire work, allied to his heuristic notion of a "creative hermeneutics," not merely fits but exemplifies the central contemporary concerns of post-Romantic hermeneutics. Indeed, Eliade's work challenges contemporary hermeneutics at exactly the point where it most needs challenge—namely, on the concept of the "other" in all Western hermeneutical work.

Part of the reason why such a study may be valuable is that some critics of Eliade's work have, in effect, misread his work as exemplifying a Romantic hermeneutics of "empathy" and "divination." Such a claim is true, of course, of Schleiermacher and Dilthey and, in the history of religions, of Eliade's predecessor, Joachim Wach. It is also true that Eliade, with typical generosity, often refers to his Romantic predecessors in hermeneutics and sometimes uses language reminiscent of theirs. Yet, Eliade's own work was not an exercise in Romantic hermeneutics at all. On the contrary, his work remains one of the great twentieth-century examples of hermeneutics as genuine conversation with the other. Eliade was, from the very beginning, one of the masters of modern hermeneutics *avant la lettre*.

Eliade and a Hermeneutics of Creativity
in the Interpretation of Religion

There is probably no problem on the contemporary intellectual scene in which there seems less consensus than on the question of the interpretation of religion. In spite of this lack of general consensus on religion, there also exists a widely-shared belief among both scholars and the wider public that Mircea Eliade is, without doubt, one of the few truly great twentieth-century interpreters of religion. There are many well-known reasons for this extraordinary achievement and fame:[5] Eliade's exceptional erudition across the traditions; his grand hypothesis of the existence of a cosmic religiosity and thereby a dialectic of the sacred and the profane in all the religions; his rare union of the erudition of a great scholar with the gifts of a major artist and thinker, a man of wide learning in religious studies as well as a man of both classical and contemporary culture. Yet there is another reason as well. Eliade proved a master of the rarest of arts—the art of interpretation of the process of interpretation itself through his interpretations of the most complex of all cultural realities—that phenomenon our culture so easily names "religion."

Indeed, religion as a phenomenon is extraordinarily difficult to interpret insofar as religion radicalizes, intensifies, and often transgresses the boundaries of those other central human phenomena to which religion is necessarily related (art, science, metaphysics, ethics, and politics). To interpret religion one must also, consciously or unconsciously, interpret these other phenomena in order to understand the difference which is specifically religious. To read the creative interpreters of religion in the modern period alone is to find a pluralism that suggests a seemingly indeterminate creativity of interpretation of any religion, both by religious

---

[5] Besides Eliade's major scholarly works cited above, see also Mircea Eliade, *The Quest* (Chicago: University of Chicago Press, 1969); *The Sacred and the Profane: The Nature of Religion* (New York: Harper, 1961); *The Myth of the Eternal Return* (Princeton: Princeton University Press, 1954).

believers and by scholarly interpreters. To read contemporary works in religious studies (or even to read one issue of one of the major journals or attend one session of one of the major conferences of scholars in the field) is to recognize a radical pluralism, indeed an intense conflict of interpretations, from which there can often seem no honorable exit.

The clearest expression of that creativity is the pluralism of interpretation itself. Within that pluralism, how is it possible for the wider community of inquiry to consent upon the better and the worse, the truly creative interpreters and the mere "bright ideas" among the various contenders? The turn to interpretation-theory among many scholars in religious studies who have followed Eliade's way of a creative hermeneutics of the "other" may provide the best way to encourage creativity in interpretation without forfeiting the need for criteria of adequacy for all interpretation.

Indeed the notorious difficulty of even defining religion in a manner that does not exclude some religious phenomenon is merely the first indication of the difficulty. Western definitions of religion have become so contested that some historians of religion have suggested that we drop the word "religion" altogether and substitute some less Western-oriented word like "faiths" or "traditions" or "ways."[6] Yet before accepting this kind of radical linguistic surgery, it seems wise to try to describe the plurality of the religious phenomenon even before trying to define it. This option seems a responsible communal task insofar as it will allow for some initial description of the *de facto* pluralism of interpretations. It will, for example, allow us to recognize the empirical wisdom in the remark of a historian of religion colleague of mine at a recent conference, "I can't define religion, but I know it when I see it."[7] So, I suspect, do we all. But the fact is we know (or we

[6] See Wilfred Cantwell Smith, *The Meaning and End of Religion* (New York: New American Library, 1963); John Cobb, "The Religions," in Peter C. Hodgson and Robert H. King, eds., *Christian Theology* (Philadelphia: Fortress, 1982), pp. 299-322.

[7] I owe this comment to my esteemed colleague, Wendy Doniger, whose studies of myths as well as "otherness" are exemplary in their sensitivity to the

think we know) several possibly complementary, possibly contra-
dictory, phenomena.

In the ordinary language sense of the term, when we call
something religious we ordinarily mean a perspective expressing a
dominating interest in certain universal and elemental features of
human existence as those features bear on the human desire for
liberation and authentic existence (V. Harvey). In the further
sense of the term "religion" used in contemporary religious
studies, we can refer, first, to the pluralism of ways of being
religious. To suggest a first and obvious pluralism: within most
major religions there are in fact several ways to be religious. Such
familiar contrast terms as the prophetic-ethical trajectory of a
religion as distinct from the mystical-metaphysical-aesthetic trajectory in the same religion or such classic religious types as
prophet or reformer as distinct from priest, sage, and mystic are
sufficient indications that, within most religions, there exists a
plurality of ways of being religious. Indeed one of the most
important conversations within a particular religion is the never-
ending debate on what is the predominant character of that
religion. For example, the startling scholarly discoveries of Gershom Scholem of the kabbalistic-mystical traditions in Judaism
have complicated earlier discussions of the prophetic-ethical
"core" of Judaism as a religion.[8]

Indeed, as prospective interpreters move from interpreting the
pluralistic ways of being religious within their own tradition to
the radically pluralistic ways of the great religions (and the
pluralism within each), they are much more likely to recognize
the need for developing hermeneutical criteria that can enhance
the possibilities of a responsible interpretation of religious plura-

issues of this book. See Wendy Doniger O'Flaherty, *Other People's Myths* (New
York: Harper & Row, 1989).

[8] Gershom Scholem, *On the Kabbalah and Its Symbolism* (New York:
Schocken, 1969); see also Moshe Idel, *Kabbalah: New Perspectives* (New Haven:
Yale University Press, 1988); and on mysticism in all three monotheistic tradi-
tions, see Moshe Idel and Bernard McGinn, eds., *Mystical Union and Monotheistic
Faith: An Ecumenical Dialogue* (New York: Macmillan, 1989).

lism. Any initial recognition of the pluralism within each religion intensifies, when interpreters of religion focus upon some *one* phenomenon within the religion. For within each of the great ways of being religious, there are in fact several candidates for focus. Consider, for example, how important a choice is made when an interpreter (like most philosophers or theologians) chose some phenomenon of religious thought (like religious "doctrines") as the central clue to the religion. Then the analysis of the cognitive status of beliefs, doctrines, myths, symbols, becomes the crucial and sometimes the sole test-case for interpreting the religion.

As Eliade makes clear, this choice of "thought" or "doctrine" as the religious reality chosen for analysis by most philosophers and theologians confines the study of religion, from the very beginning, within too narrow boundaries. As Eliade's great work *The History of Religious Ideas* demonstrates, even Hegel's ambitious *Philosophy of Religion* is too limited in its scope to a few religious cultures when a true phenomenology of the religious spirit would demand an analysis of all the great religious cultures. Most especially, we now know, thanks to Eliade, that we must interpret the archaic cultures and the archaic strands in our own culture - those strands which the philosophers and theologians, Hegel first among them, either ignored or claimed, too easily and too soon, had already been sublated by the so-called "higher religions."[9] And yet even this problem of a failure of scope in Western philosophy and theology, as Eliade's great earlier companion volume, *Patterns of Comparative Religion*, makes clear, is not merely a problem of historical coverage or quantitative range. Indeed, here Eliade's brilliant choice of Goethe as a model rather than Hegel finds its true fruit. The need, he saw early, was not first for a history but for a morphology of the

[9] As the recent editions of Hegel's *Lectures on the Philosophy of Religion* show, however, Hegel was far more open to change in his own position on the "religions" than previously interpreted. He continued to study and change on the issue. See, especially, volume 2, *Determinate Religion*, of Hegel's *Lectures*, ed. Peter C. Hodgson (Berkeley: University of California Press, 1987).

primordial religious forms. How may the classic religious forms be arranged and thereby allow their meaning to be analyzed? How may we find not merely the historical origins of the great religions, but the primordial religious events of some manifestation of the cosmos at the origin of all the religions? How can we rediscover the meaningful unity of the human with the cosmos as that unity is disclosed in every hierophany of the sacred from the cosmic tree of the archaic peoples through the cross of Christianity? And how can we do this in such manner that we can hermeneutically acknowledge, through an interpretation more like Goethe's than Hegel's, that the original bud (or primordial revelation) will "bloom" in a thousand different ways dependent upon the ever-changing existential situation of "homo religiosus?"

Like Hegel, but more radically and expansively, Eliade insists that the full range of the human spirit in all its historical manifestations must be studied if we are ever to develop a true phenomenology of the human spirit — thus the great volumes of *The History of Religious Ideas*. Like Goethe, but less confined than Goethe was to the classical culture of Greece, Eliade developed his morphology by showing how, beyond and before Homer and Hesiod, Plato and Aristotle, and the whole Mediterranean classical culture of our Western tradition, lies the great archaic roots of that culture and all cultures and all religions from Asia through Oceania and the Americas, through Europe and Africa: hence *The Patterns of Comparative Religion*. In Eliade's creative hermeneutics, both morphology and history unite in all his individual works on shamanism, yoga, alchemy, witchcraft, hermeticism, mysticism, Australian aboriginal religion and the camouflages of the sacred in our own profane world: in science fiction, in the interest in occultism and communes, in the fascination of modern youth with the religious traditions of the East, in dreams, in new myths, in sexuality, in rock music and films.

Perhaps one can also suggest that through his profound universalism Eliade is also most profoundly particular, that is,

Rumanian:[10] for the remarkable and diverse culture of Rumania, at once Latin and Slavic, at a crossroads between East and West, at once urban and, in Eliade's youth, with firm rural grounding in the archaic traditions through its rich folklore and folk traditions, freed Eliade to see the need for a new phenomenology of the spirit beyond Hegel. This Rumanian heritage produced a new universality in Eliade—just as Hegel in the midst of the battle of Jena was inspired to write his intense conflict-filled phenomenology, a *Bildungs-Roman* of *Geist* itself; just as Goethe, in the calm oasis of a charmed Weimar, was inspired to write his calm and classical morphology of all plant life. As Eliade's work on the religious classics shows, the intensification of one's own particular culture is the route to true universality. His deep Rumanian roots, I believe, freed him to become the one modern interpreter of religion who could unite both morphology and history in a manner that illuminated both. Thus did Eliade need to create a new hermeneutics of religion which would bear remarkable similarities to the most advanced theoretical reflections in modern hermeneutical theory and theological hermeneutics informed by the inter-religious dialogue.

Within the pluralism of candidates for study within any religion (ideas, rituals, myths, symbols, sacred texts) each interpreter must first try to find which major creative phenomenon can illuminate the whole. In Eliade's case, he dared to interpret all those phenomena and illuminated the meaning of each by its relationship to the others. Above all, as in the interpretation of art, Eliade insisted that the interpreter of religion needs to locate and interpret not the period-pieces of the religion but the classics, those original religious expressions of the sacred which remain highly particular in both origin and expression but which disclose the universal reality of the religious as the manifestation of the cosmos and, ultimately, of Being Itself.

By focusing major attention on the interpretation of all the

[10]On Eliade's Rumanian roots, see Mac Linscott Ricketts, *Mircea Eliade: the Romanian Roots, 1907-1945*, 2 vols. (New York: Columbia University Press, 1988).

religious classics in all the religions, moreover, we may also come to believe, with Eliade, that interpretation-theory[11] may hold a singular clue to understanding this elusive phenomenon of religion. For interpretation-theory both encourages creativity and demands criteria of adequacy. Morphology and history unite, in Eliade's work, to become not only a hermeneutics of religion, but a new model for hermeneutics itself.

If we are willing to risk an interpretation of these religious classics,[12] moreover, we will also recognize as contemporary interpreters that the risk is inevitably great. How great that risk is can be seen with full force in Eliade's published journals where he writes of his existential struggle, even at times, his genuine terror, in the face of his attempts to understand the radically other, for example, such religious phenomena as Aztec human sacrifice or cannibalism. To read those journals, in fact, is to acknowledge how radical the problem of otherness becomes when it ceases to be only a philosophical category or, as in Western hermeneutics, only Western in scope and interest. Instead the true otherness becomes a personally appropriated meaning of what was once merely outside the interpreter as radically other. Indeed, Eliade's very notion of "creative hermeneutics" radicalizes the notion of "otherness" prevalent in Western hermeneutics by insisting that the most intense forms of otherness are the archaic rituals, myths, and practices of the "others" (those many still misname the "primitives") as well as the camouflaged remnants of an archaic otherness in ourselves—in our dreams, terrors, desires, camouflaged myths, and ordinary, even banal, rituals of the everyday where the sacred now hides. These archaic "others" must be allowed to enter our consciousness by entering through both the

[11] See Hans-Georg Gadamer, *Truth and Method* (New York: Seabury, 1975); Paul Ricoeur, *Hermeneutics and the Human Sciences*, ed., J. B. Thompson (Cambridge: Cambridge University Press, 1981); *Interpretation Theory: Discourse and the Surplus of Meaning* (Fort Worth, TX: Texas Christian University Press, 1976).

[12] For an analysis of the category "classic," see David Tracy, *The Analogical Imagination: Christian Theology and the Culture of Pluralism* (New York: Crossroad, 1981), pp. 99-154.

unconscious and the "transconscious" reality manifested explicitly in Yoga and shamanism and manifested as well in the ordinary myths and rituals of all great religions. For as Eliade teaches us, the religious phenomenon is inevitably a profoundly ambiguous phenomenon of otherness in both human thought and history. Religion is cognitively ambiguous precisely as a manifestation of the Other: of Being, the cosmos, the sacred that both reveals and withdraws itself in all the religions.

Moreover, this cognitive ambiguity of religion is more than equalled in human action by a pervasive sense of the otherness of the moral ambiguity of religion as well. Religions release not only creative possibilities for the good in individuals, societies, and cultures but also (and sometimes at the same time) frightening, even demonic realities—as the tragedy at Jonestown disclosed anew. Yet this cognitive and ethical ambiguity of religion, this creative disclosure of both the true and the false, the good and the evil, even the beyond good and evil possibilities of the "holy" and the "demonic," should be sufficient evidence to warrant the belief that religion is an intrinsically pluralistic and ambiguous phenomenon of otherness that radically tests any hermeneutic theory. The turn to modern interpretation-theory, and Eliade's contribution to it, may help us see this seeming truism with greater clarity.

Interpretation Theory:
Creativity and the Pluralism of Readings

Interpretation as a problem or even as an explicit issue becomes a central issue in cultural periods of crisis. So it was for the Stoics and their reinterpretation of the Greek and Roman myths. So it is for Jews and Christians since the emergence of historical consciousness. The sense of distance that any contemporary Westerner may feel in relationship to the classics of Western culture impels the contemporary interest in the process of interpretation. If, however, as Eliade insisted, we focus only on our sense of historical distance from the classics of our culture as well as our sense of cultural parochialism exposing our inability to interpret the classics of other cultures, we are likely to formulate the problem of interpretation as primarily a problem of avoiding misunderstanding. Even Schleiermacher, justly credited as the "founder" of modern hermeneutics, often tended to formulate the problem of hermeneutics in this manner. One aspect of Schleiermacher's mixed discourse in hermeneutics (his emphasis on empathy and divination) tended to encourage the development of Romantic hermeneutics. The other aspect of Schleiermacher's hermeneutics (his emphasis on developing methodical controls to avoid misunderstanding) tended to encourage the development of strictly methodological (first historicist, then formalist) controls.

The fruits of the impasse occasioned by that mixed discourse remain with us yet. For many theories of interpretation, the central insight is still the actuality of historical and cultural distance: hence, our sense of "alienation" from both our own classics and the classics of other cultures. The central problem then becomes the need to avoid misunderstanding and the central hope lies in the controls afforded by some methodology (usually either historical or formalist) to keep us from forcing these alien texts of alien cultures or earlier periods of our own culture into the alien and alienating horizon of our present narrow self-understanding.

It is impossible in so short a space to develop the complex and still ongoing debates on hermeneutics in the modern period. For the moment, I can only hope to clarify my own position and the enormous contribution which Eliade's hermeneutics of religion makes for hermeneutics itself. As my previous remarks suggest and as I have tried to defend in written work elsewhere,[13] I do not believe that either of the two principal strands on hermeneutics bequeathed to us by Schleiermacher's creative and, indeed, classic reflections on interpretation is adequate. More exactly, the interpreter as empathizing, divinizing virtuoso (or genius) is a Romantic legacy that has yielded some fruit. Yet basically purely

[13] See David Tracy, *Plurality and Ambiguity: Hermeneutics, Religion, and Hope* (San Francisco: Harper & Row, 1987).

Romantic notions of creativity and imagination yield the kind of intellectual havoc that has given creativity a bad name in many circles. Moreover, the hope for methodological controls (either historicist or formalist) that will "guarantee" correct understanding seems seriously misplaced. Those controls, to be sure, do help all interpreters to avoid serious (e.g., anachronistic) misunderstandings of ancient texts, and often help us to reconstruct the authentic text needing interpretation. Above all, historical consciousness rouses our consciousness of both the classic's and our own historicity. But the belief that, by avoiding a-historicist misunderstanding, we also somehow achieve understanding of the questions and responses of the classics seems mistaken. This is surely the central insistence of modern hermeneutics since Heidegger and Gadamer and is, as well, the central contribution of Eliade to working out the most difficult type of hermeneutics of all: a hermeneutics of that most puzzling of phenomena, religion. For it can justly be said that by introducing his radical category of the religious, archaic "other," Eliade developed a hermeneutics of religion that both confirmed and challenged modern post-Romantic Western hermeneutics.

In the first step of hermeneutics,[14] every interpreter enters the task of interpretation with some pre-understanding of the subject-matter of the phenomenon requiring interpretation. Historical consciousness helps to clarify the complex reality of the interpreter's pre-understanding. If the expression "historicity" is not merely an ontological abstraction, it bespeaks the other truth missed by Enlightenment polemics against "prejudgments" and "traditions," as both Gadamer and Eliade insist. The fact is that no interpreter enters into the attempt to understand any text without pre-judgments formed by the history of the effects of her/his culture. No interpreter, in fact, is as purely autonomous as the Enlightenment model promised. The recognition of tradition

---

[14] This section is an interpretation and rendering of Hans-Georg Gadamer's famous analysis of interpretation on the models of the game and dialogue in *Truth and Method*, pp. 80-146; 235-345.

means that every interpreter enters into the act of interpretation bearing the history of the effects, both conscious and preconscious, of the traditions to which we ineluctably belong. As Gadamer insists, we belong to the history of these effects of our traditions—that is, we belong to history and language far more than history or language belong to us.

Yet the fact that we say that the interpreter "enters" the process of interpretation also allows us to recognize that a second step in that process occurs. The clearest way to see this second step is to consider the reality of our experience of any classic text, image, symbol, event, ritual, or person.

When interpreting any *classic* in any tradition, for example, we may note that these texts or rituals or myths or symbols bear a certain permanence and excess of meaning that resists a "definitive" interpretation. Our experience of the classic vexes, provokes, elicits a claim to serious attention. Precisely this claim to attention from the classic provokes our own pre-understanding into a dual recognition: an acknowledgment of how "formed" our preunderstanding is and, at the same time, a recognition of the "vexing," or "provocation" elicited by the claim to attention of this classic as other.

Recall, for example, Eliade's masterful description, in his autobiography, of how his experience of India as a young man helped him both to discover the claim to attention of the great classics of that extraordinary culture upon him and, at the same time, freed him to rediscover the archaic roots of all cultures. This rediscovery began with his recovery of the significance of the folk-traditions of his native Rumania. It expanded to the latent, forgotten, often repressed, archaic roots of our own classical Mediterranean culture. Through India, therefore, Eliade discovered not only India; he also rediscovered Rumania. Through Rumania, he taught the rest of us to move beyond our fascination with the classical Greece of Hegel, Goethe, Nietzsche, Heidegger, and Gadamer and thereby rediscover the archaic roots of Greece itself. Thus could Eliade unite Greek classical culture (and thereby ourselves) to the whole Indo-European archaic world.

This discovery of a latent archaic otherness in classical cultures, in turn, freed Eliade to note all the "others" beyond even that expanded world: from Siberian shamans, to Yogins, to Australian aborigines, to the great African traditions, to the religions of the native Americas, to the Hermetic and Kabbalistic traditions in the West. He taught Jewish and Christian theologians to discover, beyond even their prophetic and Abrahamic roots, the great cosmic religiosity also present in the scriptures. He taught philosophy and theology to rethink how even the great eschatological myths of the Western religions became myths of origins where "time shall be no more." Like Hegel, he insisted that only through the other can we discover ourselves. Unlike Hegel, Eliade needed no master-slave dialectic to understand the other. He welcomed the other, the different, the many, as equals—as equal participants in the religion of the cosmos that unites all humanity and as equal participants who could teach moderns the fuller meaning of a new humanism that would finally take seriously the whole of humanity. The interpreter, for both Gadamer and Eliade, must be willing to interpret the claim to attention of the other in order to understand even the self. The actual experience of that claim to attention may range from a tentative sense of resonance with the questions posed by the classic through senses of import or even shock of recognitions or repugnance elicited by the same classic.

At this point, the interpreter may search for some heuristic model by means of which one may better understand the complex process of interaction between text and interpreter—that interaction now set in motion by the claim to attention of the text. This search for a heuristic model for the process of interpretation provides the third step in modern hermeneutics. Gadamer's now famous and controversial suggestion of the model of the "game" of conversation for this process of interpretation seems appropriate here for understanding Eliade's own hermeneutical practice with the archaic other. For the model of conversation is not imposed upon our experience of interpretation as some new *de jure* method, norm, or rule. Rather the phenomenon of conversation aptly describes anyone's *de facto* experience of interpreting any classic. To understand how this is the case, first consider the more general phenomenon of the "game" before describing the "game of conversation." The key to any game is not the self-consciousness of the players in the game but rather the release of self-consciousness into the to-and-fro, the back-and-forth, movement which constitutes the game. The attitude of the players of any game is a phenomenon dependent upon this natural back-and-forth movement in the game itself. When we really play any game it is not so much we who are playing as it is the game which plays us.

It is interesting to note that the preface to Gadamer's great work in hermeneutics, *Truth and Method*, begins with Rilke's poem on the game of the cosmos. It is even more interesting to note that precisely the rhythms of the cosmos is, for Eliade, the singular clue to what might be called the universal language-game underlying all the great cultures and religions. Through that cosmic ritual, that sacred game, humanity can learn to let-go and enter anew into the to-and-fro movement, the game, the rhythm, of the cosmos itself as that rhythm is disclosed in all the krato-phanies, hierophanies, and theophanies of the religions. Only if we cannot release ourselves to the back-and-forth movement of any game, can we not play. If we can play, then we experience ourselves as caught-up-in-the-movement of the game itself. We realize that our usual self-consciousness cannot be the key to playing. Thus, we may find, however temporarily, a sense of a new self given through our actual playing, our release to the rhythmic movement of the game of the cosmos.

The common human experience of playing a game can become the key to the basic model of hermeneutics as conversation. For what is authentic conversation (as distinct from debate, gossip, or confrontation) other than the ability to become caught up in the to-and-fro movement of the logic of question and response with the other? Anyone who was privileged to know Mircea Eliade knows how much he loved this game of civilized conversation. Anyone who has read any of the major texts in Eliade's *oeuvre* knows how willing he was to allow the claim of the radically other to challenge him into new conversation and new self-understanding. That Eliade entered into conversation with the most radical otherness of all, the manifestations, both primordial and historical, of the religions is clear to all his readers. That is the very essence of his creative hermeneutics and, indeed, of hermeneutics itself as a willingness to risk conversation with the radically other. As much as Gadamer, Eliade shows how hermeneutics is conversation with the other. Unlike Gadamer and most other Western hermeneutic theorists, Eliade developed a creative hermeneutics as a conversation with the radically other.

The "archaic" ontology[15] articulated by Eliade as the "other" we most need to interpret becomes the focal meaning for understanding religion as an eruption of power in some manifestation of the whole now experienced as the sacred cosmos. The manifestation occurs preverbally,[16] in a space and a time separated from ordinary space and historical time; the ordinary now becomes the "profane;" the extraordinary becomes the sacred because of the power saturating the manifestation of the sacred in this rock, this tree, this ritual, this cosmogonic myth.

By entering the ritual, by retelling the myth, by creatively reinterpreting the symbol, we can escape from the "nightmare" of history and even the "terror" of ordinary time.[17] We can finally enter true time, the time of the repetition of the actions of the whole at the origin of the cosmos. *In illo tempore*, the power from the whole was first disclosed as sacred. That power discloses itself

[15] For two helpful studies of Eliade here, see Guilford Dudley III, *Religion on Trial: Mircea Eliade and his Critics* (Philadelphia: Temple University Press, 1977); Douglas Allen, *Structure and Creativity in Religion: Hermeneutics in Mircea Eliade's Phenomenology* (The Hague: Mouton, 1978).

[16] See Paul Ricoeur, "Manifestation and Proclamation," *The Journal of the Blaisdell Institute* 12 (Winter 1978).

[17] For Eliade, see, especially, *The Myth of the Eternal Return*. The disturbing Rumanian historical background for Eliade's famous and ambiguous reflections on the "terror of history" is analyzed in necessary historical details in the scholarly work of Ricketts, *Mircea Eliade: The Romanian Roots*, and in Ivan Strenski, *Four Theories of Myth in Twentieth Century History: Cassirer, Eliade, Lévi-Strauss, and Malinowski* (Iowa City, IA: University of Iowa Press, 1987).

to those participating in its manifestations. Only by interpreting the ritual, the symbol, the festival, the myth, can we participate in a realm disclosed on the other side of the ordinary: that realm has manifested itself as sacred, has exposed the ordinary as profane. The sacred, at the same time, chooses *any* ordinary reality—this rock, this tree, this city, this mountain, this rite—as the medium for a disclosure of power—the *axis mundi*, the sacred mountain, the cosmic tree, the rites of initiation, the rituals which free us by their very repetitions to enter the sacred time of the origins of the cosmos.

By interpreting the great manifestations of the sacred, Eliade teaches us to seek "no more souvenirs" from the ordinary and to acknowledge the truth that "*only* the paradigmatic is the real." Here we find the paradigmatic, not in the disappointments of ordinary time and history, not even in the recovered time of Proust, but in the otherness of the ahistorical, atemporal time of repetition in the archaic myths, rituals, symbols, and images of the true time of the origins of the cosmos. Eliade finds this reality of manifestation alive in the West mainly in rural cultures. But even in urban settings, he shows how the traces of the cosmic live in the liturgies of Judaism and Christianity, in the archetypal dreams of the night, in the ecstasy of sexual expression, in the disturbing underflow of the unconscious, in the desperation of our fascination with fantasy, astrology, alchemy, science fiction and the "East" we insist on calling "mysterious," and the archaic cultures we insist on labelling "primitive." In his words of literature, moreover, Eliade joined many of the great modernist artists—Faulkner, Joyce, Eliot, Pound, Picasso, Ionesco, Stravinsky—in their move away from the banalities and terrors of history in a search for some ahistorical, atemporal myth which may yet save us.

More than any contemporary Western thinker, Eliade articulated—through his scholarship, his constructive ontology, his creative hermeneutics, and his art—[18] what the reality of a participa-

[18] See, especially, his novel, *The Forbidden Forest* (Notre Dame, IN: University of Notre Dame Press, 1978).

tion in the cosmos as the sacred might be: a participation familiar, I believe, in ordinarily more muted tones to be sure, to any genuinely religious experience and expression, including the modern Christian and Jew.

No single Western thinker seems as able as Eliade is at disclosing this radical sense of belonging to, even saturation by, the rhythms of the cosmos, the whole, as a sacred power. Moreover no contemporary thinker seems as able to challenge our usual Western Augustinian assumptions as does Eliade with his extraordinary retrieval of the genius of Orthodox Christianity: a theology oriented to and from not history and ethos, but the cosmos and aesthetics; a style of religious practice oriented not so much by the word of scripture as by the manifestations of the sacred in image, icon, ritual, logos and cosmological theologies; a way of being Christian that demands both radical separation from the ordinary via the rituals and myths of the repetition of the origins of the cosmos and allows participation in the manifestations of the sacred available to our now "divinized" humanity.

It is an extraordinary legacy Mircea Eliade has bequeathed us. It is a legacy which allows, indeed forces us to pay attention to the archaic other.[19] In seeking dialogue with the archaic other, we need to pay attention to the archaic traditions alive in our world as well as to remember our own repressed archaic heritage. The archaic is other but must not be allowed to be merely a projected other. Its memory lives even now in us: memory heals, memory liberates, memory manifests the power and rhythms of the sacred cosmos itself—that cosmos the archaic traditions can teach us to see anew with the always youthful eyes of their always healing memory.

---

[19] For two examples of critical developments of Eliade's work here, see Charles Long, *Significations: Signs, Symbols and Images in the Interpretation of Religion* (Philadelphia: Fortress, 1986), and Lawrence Sullivan, *Icanchus' Drum: An Orientation to Meaning in South American Religions* (New York: Macmillan, 1988).

THE BUDDHIST-CHRISTIAN DIALOGUE

Post-Modernity and Buddhism

The Buddhist-Christian dialogue has proved to be one of the most puzzling and fruitful attempts at genuine dialogue in our period. It is an exceptionally fruitful dialogue insofar as the reality of the other as other is acknowledged as at the heart of all true dialogue. For the Christian or Jew what can be more other than this Buddhist other who names Ultimate Reality not God but Emptiness? This other who declares that there is no self or, more exactly, with Nāgārjuna, that both self and no-self neither exist nor do not exist? This Buddhist other who employs a highly metaphysical vocabulary and insists on the need for correct thinking while at the same time suspecting all metaphysical and, at the limit, all language? This other who insists that the familiar Western analogical and dialectical languages of philosophy and theology are unable to rid Western thought of the dualisms that allegedly distort all our thought (subject-object, history-nature, transcendence-immanance, body-soul, other-self)? At the same time, Buddhist thinkers often employ brilliant dialectical strategies (as in Nāgārjuna) or develop analogical relationships (as in Nishitani) in order to insist upon a non-dialectical and non-analogical non-dualism.[1] For healing, even salvific, insight

---

[1] In Nāgārjuna, for a representative text, see *Mūlamadhyamikakārikā* (Tokyo: Hokusseido Press, 1970). On Nāgārjuna, see Frederich Streng, *Emptiness* (Nashville: Abingdon, 1967); David Kalupahana, *Nāgārjuna: The Philosophy of the Middle Way* (Albany: State University of New York Press, 1986); Andrew P. Tuck, *Comparative Philosophy and the Philosophy of Scholarship: On the Western Interpretation of Nāgārjuna* (New York: Oxford University Press, 1990); see also Nāgārjuna, *Vigrahavyāvartanī*, trs. in K. Bhattacharya, *The Dialectical Method of Nāgārjuna* (New Delhi: Motilal Banarsidass, 1978); Étienne Lamotte, *Le Traité de la grande vertu de sagesse de Nāgārjuna* V (Louvain: Université de Louvain, 1980). For Nishitani, see Keyi Nishitani, *Religion and Nothingness* (Berkeley: University of California Press, 1983).

consists, for the Buddhist, in recognizing all reality as neither one nor many but as not-two (non-duality).

A more "other" form of thought than Buddhist thought on God and self, on history and nature, indeed, on thought itself (including dialogical thought) would be difficult to conceive for Western Christians with our different strategies and categories of philosophical and theological thought. Even process thought cannot but finally acknowledge Buddhist thought as radically other.[2] For however great the affinities between a process understanding of all reality as constituted by internal relations to the Buddhist understanding of reality as constituted by radical dependent origination, the differences are equally clear. For Whitehead, there is both teleology and order to the unending relational process; hence a teleological order is needed in order to understand the relational process of creativity itself. For process theology, there is, above all, the necessity for order, yielding the process, di-polar God who orders reality. For John Cobb, moreover, the Buddhist understanding of no-self needs the process notion of the emergence of creative possibility in human freedom if that elusive Buddhist notion would ever prove acceptable to Christian theological thought as Christian. But once the process category of freedom enters the Buddhist understanding of the true freedom of the "true" self as untimately no-self, such agential process freedom must be frankly disavowed on inner-Buddhist terms.

Other thinkers like Langdon Gilkey[3] have suggested that the nearest analogue in Western thought is neither Whitehead nor Hegel but a radical, non-reductionist process-like form of naturalism like that of John Dewey. For in Deweyan naturalism all

---

[2] See John B. Cobb, Jr., *Beyond Dialogue: Toward a Mutual Transformation of Christianity and Buddhism* (Philadelphia: Fortress, 1982), pp. 145-51.

[3] Gilkey's important Christian theological reflections on the Buddhist-Christian dialogue will be collected into a separate volume. For one example, see Langdon Gilkey, "The Mystery of Being and Nonbeing," in *Society and the Sacred* (New York: Crossroad, 1981), pp. 123-39. Gilkey's insight into the similarity and contrast of Deweyan and Buddhist thought is particularly illuminating.

reality is reality-in-process but a process more like the Buddhists' than like Whitehead's: without God and without restriction. And yet even here the differences from Buddhism become clear. Neither Dewey's trust in scientific method nor the democratic implications Dewey construed in the naturalistic process view of reality are shared by most Buddhist thinkers. Rather, as Nishitani makes clear,[4] for the Buddhist thinker, both the modern naturalist's trust in scientific method and any naturalist belief in a *telos* to the social-political process cannot but prove another illustration of the Western law of infinite desire. Once its *telos* is exposed as an illusion, the desparate law of infinite desire leads to a nihility that masks an ultimate nihilism. Western humanist nihilism cannot disclose the true Buddhist realization of the Nothingness that finally dissolves the law of infinite desire by enlightening and liberating the compulsive ego-self from its desire to realize the no-self of sunyata.

My own belief is that the nearest affinity to Buddhist thought (or, more exactly, to the Mahayana Buddhism of Nāgārjuna as that radical form of Buddhism is rethought in contemporary terms by the modern Kyoto school of Nishida, Tanabe, Nishitani, Takeyushi, Abe and others)[5] is to be found in neither Hegel nor Whitehead nor Dewey but in certain contemporary strands of post-modern thought, like that of Gilles Deleuze and Jacques Derrida.[6] Perhaps the greatest affinity between much French

---

[4] Nishitani, *Religion and Nothingness*, .

[5] On the Kyoto School, see Fritz Buri, *Der Buddha-Christus als des Herr des wahren Selbst: Die Religionphilosophie der Kyoto Schule und das Christentum* (Stuttgart: Paul Haupt, 1982); and Frederich Franck, ed., *The Buddha Eye: An Anthology of the Kyoto School* (New York: Crossroad, 1982). For representative individual studies, see Masao Abe, *Zen and Western Thought*, ed., William La Fleur (Honolulu: University of Hawaii Press, 1985); Kitaro Nishida, *Intelligibility and the Philosophy of Nothingness* (New York: Greenwood Press, 1973); and Hayime Tanabe, *Philosophy as Metanoetics* (Berkeley: University of California Press, 1987). I wish to express my thanks to James Fredericks for introducing me to the study of Tanabe. Frederick's dissertation on Rahner and Tanabe (University of Chicago, 1988) will be published in book form.

[6] For some suggestive comparisons of Derrida and Nāgārjuna, see Robert Magliola, *Derrida on the Mend* (West Lafayette, IN: Purdue University Press, 1986); for representative Derrida here, see Jacques Derrida, *Spurs: Nietzsche's*

deconstructive and Kyoto Buddhist thought is the common insistence on the illusionary character of the self and thereby of any modern Western attempt to use that self to ground or provide a foundation for "reality." This critique of the logocentism (with Derrida) or the onto-theo-logical character of all Western philosophy and theology (with Heidegger) or the "foundationalism" of Western transcendental and metaphysical enterprises (with Rorty) is remarkably similar to the strangely metaphysical, yet anti-metaphysical, character of much contemporary Buddhist thought. Moreover, Derrida and Deleuze, with their distinct but related notions of difference and their critique of all dialectics as disallowing difference by rendering differences as dialectical oppositions, joined to their insistence on the undecidability of all meaning through our need to use language, bear some remarkable family resemblances to Nāgārjuna's anti-dialectical yet dialectical insistence of the undecidability of all thought-in-language. Yet even here, a new difference—now on the notion of difference itself—emerges. For any Buddhist notion of "not-two" (non-duality) seems lacking in both Deleuze's sheer celebration of Nietzschean difference and Derrida's merging of difference and deferral to yield radically undecidable *différence* and dissemination. The anti-dialectics of the deconstructionists celebrate difference and the anti-dialectical dialectics of the Kyoto school signal non-duality.

At the same time, the emphasis on the epiphanic character of archaic thought in, for example, Eliade or Jung may suggest a remarkable similarity between the primal sense of manifestation of the cosmos in the great archetypes of all the traditions. That same sense of truth as manifestation emerges, in more muted tones, in the "epiphanic" moments of the great literary modernists: the involuntary memory of Marcel Proust, the luminous moments of Virginia Woolf, the epiphanies of James Joyce. It is

Style (Chicago: University of Chicago Press, 1979), and *Margins of Philosophy* (Chicago: University of Chicago Press, 1983). For Deleuze, see Gilles Deleuze, *Nietzsche and Philosophy* (New York: Columbia University Press, 1983).

hardly surprising that someone like Eliade or Jung would be
attracted to the great literary modernists and to Hinduism more
than Buddhism, as an alternative to contemporary, history-
oriented, dialectical Western thought. The post-moderns, however, have quite different affinities. In both philosophy (as in
Derrida and Deleuze), in Lacanian anti-ego psychology and anti-
Jungian psychoanalysis, and in most post-modern literature, even
the transient epiphanies of the great literary modernists are now
gone. Indeed post-modern thought wishes to dissolve all modernist epiphanies as surely as Buddhist thought dissolves the great
archetypes of presence of the archaic traditions and the "true
self" of Vedanta where "*Brahman and Atman are one.*" Like the
Buddhists' attack on Vedantic thought,[7] the post-moderns reject
every form of presence—now labelled pejoratively logocentrism
and foundationalism—in Western literature and philosophy.
Hegel's dialectic of God and even Heidegger's event of disclosure-
concealment become the other to Derrida, as surely as Derrida is
the other to every Hegelian and every thinker of presence. In
Eastern thought, the same struggle continues: witness the enduring clash between the descendants of Shankara and those of
Nāgārjuna.

For Western thought on other cultures and traditions always
reveals more about itself than about the other when it insists
upon its affinities to the thought of some preferred other. Recall
the readings of China of our seventeenth- and eighteenth-century
predecessors (like Leibniz and Voltaire after they had read the
letters of the Jesuit missionaries) in their clearly enlightenment
versions of classical neo-Confucianism. Recall the Romantics and
their re-discovery of themselves in their discoveries of India and
the great archaic traditions. We may be witnessing in our period
a similar sense of felt affinity between certain forms of Western
post-modern thought and certain forms of East Asian Mahayana

---

[7] See Eliot Deutsch, *Advaita Vedanta: A Philosophical Reconstruction* (Honolulu: East-West Center Press, 1969); and Mervyn Sprung, ed., *The Problem of Two
Truths in Buddhism and Vedanta* (Dordrecht: D. Reidel, 1974).

Buddhism. Whether these new post-modern versions of that Buddhist other is any more accurate than our predecessors' versions of Confucianism, Hinduism, and the archaic traditions remains a troubling and perhaps, at present, an unanswerable question.

For, just as in the case of Eliade's hermeneutics of the other, so too here in the Buddhist-Christian dialogue, the acknowledgement of how *other* the Buddhist way of practice and thought is to the Christian way of thought and practice does not guarantee an understanding of that Buddhist otherness. With Levinas, all dialogue partners must begin with a facing of the other as radically other and as critically demanding. Indeed, in my own four-year experience of the Buddhist-Christian dialogue, I have learned something of the fuller meaning of Levinas' insistence on the terror of otherness. At the same time and, in however tenuous a manner, the dialogue partner (now understood more in Gadamer's and Eliade's terms than in Levinas') must try to allow the process and challenge of mutual questioning to take over. For there is no genuine dialogue without the willingness to risk all one's present self-understanding in the presence of the other— whether that other be the text of Nagarjuna or the serene face and probing thought of one's contemporary Buddhist dialogue-partner.

It may be possible, as suggested above, to develop an analogical imagination for and by means of interreligious dialogue.[8] But any such hope demands three elements: a self-respect (which includes, of course, a respect for, even a reverence for, one's own tradition or way); a self-exposure to the other as other; and a willingness to risk all in the questioning and inquiry that constitutes the dialogue itself. In that sense, a theologian enters the Buddhist-Christian dialogue not as a cultural anthropologist nor even as a philosopher but as a committed Christian theologian. Thus have I found myself profoundly challenged by the Buddhist way. Part of that challenge has led me to take more seriously

[8] David Tracy, *The Analogical Imagination: Christian Theology and the Culture of Pluralism* (New York: Crossroad, 1981), pp. 446-457.

certain forms of Western post-modern thought and their philosophical critiques of both classical dialectical and analogical modes of thought. A more important part of that Buddhist challenge has been less cultural and philosophical than more strictly Christian theological. To try to think the initially unthinkable thoughts of no-self for the self, of emptiness for ultimate reality—and pervading both, of co-dependent origination as describing all reality— is a deeply disorienting matter, for any Christian who holds her/ his profound trust in and loyalty to the one God and therefore a belief in a responsible self disclosed by that God's self-disclosure in Sinai, Exodus, and Jesus Christ. One finds, at the beginning, that one can barely conceive what might be meant by the Buddhist; so initially other, even alien, is the thought of sunyata.

The Buddhist Challenge of the Self and Transience

Every Christian theologian sensitive to the problems of our contemporary situation and our Christian tradition enters the Buddhist-Christian dialogue with certain expectations about where one is likely to learn from and be transformed by the Buddhist conversation-partner. For example, our contemporary Western culture does suffer, at present, from the debilitating reality of possessive individualism. In such a culture, the system of individualism functions in so pervasive a way that it can turn the liberating Enlightenment notions of self-autonomy into mere individualism:[9] the self-deceptive belief in a unified, coherent, non-relational ego. Consider the havoc caused in our individual and social-political lives by the possessive individualism of this cultural understanding of the self. This sense of cultural crisis is accentuated in Western Europe and North America by a powerfully psychological culture where a reigning ego psychology can encourage notions of "maturity" and "ego-strength" as the solu-

---

[9] On the modern Western problems of the self, see Paul Ricoeur, *Soi-Même comme un autre* (Paris: Editions du Seuil, 1990); and Charles Taylor, *Sources of the Self: The Making of the Modern Identity* (Cambridge; Harvard University Press, 1989). For a sociological study, see Robert Bellah *et al.*, *Habits of the Heart* (Berkeley: University of California Press, 1985).

tion when these therapies may, in fact, be part of the culture's problem of possessive individualism. Here the Buddhist has much to teach us. Far more radically than the critique of humanism in much post-modern Western thought, more radically still than Lacan's critique of ego-psychology, the Buddhist way forces modern Westerners to confront our cultural and psychological notions of ego, self, and subject beyond the usual alternatives. An acknowledgment that our notions of ego, self, and subject are inadequate now seems a commonplace across much Western thought: recall socialist critiques of liberal individualism, Romantic and idealist notions of community and individual, as well as the classical distinctions in the Catholic social justice tradition between "individual" and "person." Yet these various and familiar Western secular, Christian, and Jewish critiques of a dominant cultural and psychological individualism, as well as philosophical critiques of the Cartesian ego or the Husserlian transcendental ego, have largely been attempts to rethink either the individual-community relationship or the philosophical relationship of the empirical ego to the transcendental ego.

Seldom in the whole history of Western philosophy or theology does as radical a position on the self as that of the Buddhist understanding of no-self occur. And yet to formulate the question in dialogue as the question of no-self is also to risk a misunderstanding of the Buddhist position. Strictly speaking, there is no Buddhist doctrine of the no-self. Rather there is a realization of emptiness and dependent co-origination and thereby no-self through such practices as Zazen meditation and occasional glimpses of this non-doctrinal truth:[10] or, as Abe formulates it in terms more familiar to Westerners, this "existential" truth. Buddhist thought, like Jewish or Christian thought, can be distinguished, but cannot be existentially separated, from its practices. Exactly here, I believe, is where the more strictly theological rather than philosophical or cultural anthropological or even history of religions perspective can be of further aid in under-

[10] Masao Abe, *Zen and Western Thought*, pp. 3-83.

standing the otherness of Buddhism. For in a strictly theological dialogue, the way and the thought (or theory and praxis) cannot ultimately be sundered. Dialogue itself is first a practice (and a difficult one) before theories on dialogue or conclusions on the results of dialogue are forthcoming.

One possible result of those Christian-Buddhist dialogues for a modern Christian can now be named: the Christian freedom of the self as no-self becomes one possible response (even Christian mystical response) to the cultural reality of possessive individualism, and allied to that possessiveness, the culture's terror of its own transience. I assume, to be sure, that Christian theology is an attempt at developing a set of mutually critical correlations between an interpretation of the tradition and an interpretation of the ever-changing situation.[11] As the cultural situation changes, the religious and theological questions evoked by the situation also change: for example, the issue of mortality in the Patristic period; the search for forgiveness in the Reformation; the search for order in the High Medieval period; the search for a notion of revelation that coheres with scientific and philosophical and cultural beliefs in liberal and modernist theologies; the questions of meaninglessness and absurdity in existentialist theologies; the shift of interest from revelation to salvation in liberation, feminist, and political theologies where the principal question becomes not the cognitive crisis of the modern unbeliever (including the unbeliever in the modern believer) but the sense of possession and massive global suffering of whole peoples and cultures. Or, as Gustavo Gutierrez nicely formulates it, for the liberation theologian, the principal question is the question not of the non-believer but of those delegated by the dominant culture to the status of non-person.

Each of these situational shifts in the principal existential and religious questions needing address have occasioned reinterpretations of the Christian tradition. Sometimes these revisions are radical ones—as in the deliteralizing of notions of "original sin"

---

[11] Tracy, *The Analogical Imagination*, pp. 47-99.

in favor of an existential analysis of how the symbol of the fall, when interpreted seriously but not literally (i.e., as referring to an historical Adam and Eve and their "fall"), is demythologized and thereby retrieved for Christian theology. Directly analogous to such Christian revisionary theologies on original sin are the kind of revisionary deliteralizing and demythologizing of the "law of karma and transmigration" that we find in such modern Buddhist thinkers as Nishitani and Abe.

At other times, the shift in religious and theological questions will occasion a new hermeneutics of suspicion on possible systemic distortions in the tradition (sexism, racism, anti-Semitism, classism, elitism). Those suspicions, in turn, will lead to various hermeneutics of retrieval of largely ignored and forgotten, sometimes even repressed, aspects of the tradition. This kind of retrieval-through-suspicion occurs when modern Christian feminist theologians retrieve aspects of the ancient goddess traditions or the wisdom-Sophia traditions or the women mystics (especially the Beguines) as providing new resources for a new Christian theology. The same kind of hermeneutical move occurs in the new theological construals of apocalyptic as an interruption of the illusory continuities of history in political theologians like Metz and Moltmann.

In my judgment, a Christian theology which takes seriously the challenge and otherness of Buddhist thought has a similar opportunity for both new suspicions and new retrievals. For if our situation is one where the question of possessive individualism (the liberalist illusion of a purely autonomous, non-relational self) strikes us as a deadly and systemic distortion of any reasonable hope for a truly Christian understanding of the self as agent, then we may well pay heed to the Buddhist radical analysis of our dilemma.

Surely the most powerful and attractive (perhaps even *fascinans et tremendum*) aspect of the Buddhist analysis of the human dilemma which appeals to any contemporary Westerner aware of the plague of possessive individualism is the Buddhist analysis of our inevitable clinging to the ego. The Augustinian understanding of the self as *curvatus in se* has certain affinities to the Buddhist insistence on the ego's compulsive clinging to itself. The Christian understanding of the self as capable of being a true, responsible self only by fidelity to the gospel dialectic of "to gain the self, one must lose the self" can be radicalized by the Buddhist notion that only by letting go of the utter unreality of the ego and its compulsive clinging can we possessive individualists break the law of the infinite desire of the compulsive ego.

To cease clinging is to cease to be an ego. At the very same time, this existential letting-go is a letting-be of a no-self whose reality *is* co-dependent origination and thereby emptiness and whose enlightened insight is at the same time into the pure "suchness" of each reality. Neither the classical Platonists with their rigorous education of desire, nor the Stoics with their courageous letting-go to all other relationships save the relationship of the Stoic self to the common *logos*, can match the radicality of the Buddhist move. Not even the classical Christian dialectic of losing the self in order to gain a true self, however transformative in relationship to the questions of anxiety, guilt, and meaninglessness, can match the Buddhist analysis of the terror of transience caused by the compulsive clinging of the ego on an individual level and even on a cultural level.

As the sense of the transience of Western culture itself becomes heightened in some post-modern notions of the radical undecidability of all our texts and traditions and the illusory foundational beliefs in self-presence in modern subjectivity from Descartes through Husserl, the Buddhist analysis of our cultural situation of possessive individualism as a situation of compulsive clinging in the face of the terror of transience cannot but increase its appeal to all post-modern Westerners. It is little wonder that Buddhism has now become not merely an Eastern option but also a Western religious option for many sensitive minds and spirits alive to the peculiarly post-modern Western sense of radical transience.

The Jew and the Christian, faithful to their prophetic heritage, continue to live the dialectic of the responsible self before the covenanting, responding God. Thus do they learn that we are freed *from* the world *for* the world. The Buddhist, in an analogous but ultimately different way, finds that enlightenment to true *nirvana* also includes the recognition that *nirvana* and *samsara* are one. For the Buddhist must not cling to the ego. The Buddhist must not even cling to non-clinging. For we should not cling to enlightenment or emptiness itself if we are to become enlightened. In an extraordinary move, unfamiliar to Platonist and Stoic alike, unfamiliar as well to classical prophetic Judaism and Christianity, the Buddhist analysis of the human dilemma suggests that the very problem (transience) becomes, for the no-self—that is, the non-clinging enlightened one—the solution. Transience as both problem and solution is a way, a way at once peculiarly Buddhist and post-modern, glimpsed by very few in the Western Christian tradition. Perhaps this way is what Ernst Troeltsch, in his unjustly neglected *Glaubenslehre*, was struggling to articulate with his profound sense of the transience of Western culture as the principal question of our late-modern theological situation.[12] Perhaps, as Christianity ceases to be a merely Eurocentric religion and becomes a truly "world church," this Buddhist insight into the religious meaning of transience may help Western Christians let go of their compulsive clinging to transient Eurocentric theological ways of thought and action.

The Christian and the Buddhist: Suspicion and Retrieval

Does the Buddhist also return to the world? In one sense, this question, which the Jew and the Christian cannot evade, becomes, for the Buddhist, a profoundly troubling question. The question may be troubling, of course, because it may be ill-formulated. For the Buddhist there is, strictly speaking, no self to return and no world to return to. But the question of some return to the world, as modern Buddhist attempts to develop a social ethics show, is a real, an existential, and a troubling question—indeed, as troubling to the modern Buddhist as the question of

[12] Ernst Troeltsch, *Glaubenslehre*

radical transience can be for the post-modern Christian. Buddhist releasement allows for a great compassion for *all* living beings after the great death of the ego. The Mahayana return to the world can only be a return of a compassionate one. Hence the Pure Land Buddhist insistence against much Zen thought that only the Boddhisattva vow is faithful to the very logic of Buddhist thought and even, with Tanabe,[13] that only "other-power" (not classical Zen self-power) is faithful to the logic of the great death and the Mahayana return. That return is a return to a world of all pervasive co-dependent origination. That return disallows both the God of classical theism and the panentheistic God of process thought securing the order and values of a world of radical relationality. That Buddhist return is also without both the teleology of modern secular thought (like Dewey's) and the eschatologies of Judaism and Christianity.

The world (if it be correct to use so structure-like a word as "world" here) of Buddhist co-dependent origination is indeed, like process thought, a world of radical relationality. For the emergence of any new occurrence is a momentary experience through the coalescence of all else. Yet, for the Buddhist, that emergence is empty of all being, substance, and form of its own. Even when a particular emergence of experience has coalesced, it achieves no existence of its own. In the very moment of arriving, the emergence also perishes. It becomes part of that radical relationality whose coalescence produces other entities. All reality is present in every entity ("suchness") and every entity pervades the whole.[14] The center is everywhere. For the Buddhist, unlike

    [13] Tanabe is, of course, atypical of the Kyoto School in this emphasis on other-power. Abe, for example, is a convert to Zen Buddhism from the other-power doctrine of Pure Land Buddhism. On Pure Land Buddhism, see Paul C. Ingram, *The Dharma of Faith: An Introduction to Classical Pure Land Buddhism* (Washington: University Press of America, 1977); and Alfred Bloom, *Shinran's Gospel of Pure Grace* (Tucson: University of Arizona Press, 1965). On the logic of the Boddhisattva, see L. Kawamura, ed., *The Boddhisattva Doctrine in Buddhism* (Waterloo, Canada: Wilfred Laurier University Press, 1981).

    [14] On the puzzling relationship of "emptiness" and "suchness" see Masao Abe, "Emptiness is Suchness," in *Zen and Western Thought*, pp. 223-31.

the process thinker, there is no circumference, no order, and no teleology. Ultimate Reality *is* emptiness.

The sense of radical transience, for those freed from the compulsive clinging to the ego (or the ego's products like a particular transient culture), becomes an enlightenment into the true emptiness of all reality. Transience is not the problem. Rather, transience is, for all those enlightened ones who have moved beyond nihilism to Emptiness and true Nothingness, the very solution to our dilemma if we would but let go. To let go of the modern possessive individual's terror of transience is to be released into transience itself as healing. A Buddhist compassion for all living beings seems to flow from that revelatory insight (where, let us note, a true revelation *is* salvation). Perhaps, as Buddhists insist, only a figure like Francis of Assisi in the West has displayed so radically a non-anthropocentric religious sense of compassion for *all* living beings. Surely our culture's dominating attitude to nature can be exposed as a compulsive clinging to an anthropocentrism by a Buddhist critique. As an ecological consciousness emerges in our culture, the Buddhist sense of radical relatedness and compassion for all living beings becomes a healing and transforming possibility.

Whether the classical prophetic sense of justice can be united to the Buddhist sense of compassion is a far more difficult question. It is also a question which modern Buddhist thinkers now valiantly struggle to answer. Many find themselves aided in this struggle by their dialogues with Jews and Christians who have tried to find better ways to relate love and justice dialectically— above all in contemporary political and liberation theologies. I, however, have neither the competence nor the right to presume to speculate on where the contemporary (especially Japanese) inner-Buddhist discussion of compassion and justice may lead.

The Buddhist-Christian dialogue may also help us to return to the radically apophatic mystical tradition, especially that of Meister Eckhart. As surely as a post-modern reader like Jacques Lacan can read Freud, so, too, a radically apophatic mystic like Meister Eckhart can help us read our prophetic texts in a post-modern time. The true God—the God of the prophets and Jesus Christ—is the one to whom we owe all our loyalty and trust. The true God can nonetheless become, through our clinging and through our refusal to let go of the law of infinite desire because of our refusal to face the radical transience which terrorizes us, merely a projected Other to whom we egoistically cling. When even prophetic denunciations of our idolatry cannot break through our compulsive clinging to an ultimately idolatrous God, then the modern Christian theologian, listening to the challenge of the Buddhist insight that belief in "God" can be the most subtle form of egoistic clinging, may rejoin Meister Eckhart and pray, "I pray to God to free me from God." The "Godhead beyond God" of Eckhart is a possible, and perhaps in the post-modern situation, even, for some, a salutary theological move for those Christians concerned to learn to live, both like and unlike the Buddhist, in a situation of radical transience where Eckhart's "Life without a why" becomes a new Christian option. Perhaps this is the sense which Thomas Merton urged upon his readers when he suggested we learn Zen meditation and attempt to become "self-transcending" Christians.

Even if the retrieval of the radically apophatic mystical reading of God and self of Meister Eckhart is possible, for the Christian if not the Buddhist, it cannot be sufficient. Here, as the distinguished Belgian-American Catholic philosopher, Louis Dupré, argues, the futher insights of Ruysbroeck must take hold.[15] For Ruysbroeck in his post-Eckhart Trinitarian mysticism, like so many in the classical Flemish tradition, had a further insight beyond Eckhart. It is the same insight which contemporary Christian theologians are attempting, now in contemporary terms, to relearn. That insight is the need for a fully mystico-prophetic contemporary Christian theology where the mystically transfor-

---

[15] Louis Dupré, *The Common Life* (New York: Crossroad, 1984), and James Wiseman's commentaries in *John Reuysbroec: The Spiritual Espousals and Other Works* (New York: Paulist, 1985). Both Dupré and Wiseman gratefully acknowledge their debt to the work of three generations of the Antwerp *Reusbroecgenootschap* (Reusbroec Society).

med self, reflecting on the profound implications of the one God as essentially Triune, returns to the world freed for life in all its earthiness and all its search for justice and love. But that return, let us note, like the Mahayana return, must be one marked by thanks and compassion—of thanks for the other of the Buddhist who, precisely through the challenge of that radical otherness, can help Christians, especially those sensitive to our contemporary situation of possessive individualism and the terror of transience, to let go, to rethink, to suspect anew, and to retrieve the forgotten mystical resources of our own tradition.

Can Mystics Read Prophetic Texts Revisited?
The Christian Neo-Platonists on the Trinity
and the Buddhist Understanding of Sunyata

Can Buddhists also help Christian theologians retrieve one neglected strand of the Christian theological tradition: the Christian neo-Platonic tradition from Pseudo-Dionysius through John Scotus Eriugena, Eckhart, Ruysbroeck, Cusanus, to important aspects of Hegel, Whitehead, Heidegger, Rahner, and Tillich?[16] This question demands further reflection. However, we need first to recall that the Christian theological tradition is, as Christian, also an interpretation of the Christian scriptures. Unlike Zen Buddhism and more like such forms of Buddhism as Tibetan, Theravadan, or even Pure Land in relationship to debates on the sutras, Christians as Christians find themselves responsible to show how their interpretations of all reality cohere with the Scriptures. Clearly this need not lead to either a fundamentalism nor even to a purely "narrativist" biblical theology,[17] as we shall see in the next chapter. This is the case, insofar as the scriptures, however prophetic and narrative they are in their core readings of God's self-manifestation in the history of Israel and the life, message, ministry, death, and resurrection of Jesus Christ, are

---

[16] For a historical-constructive study here, see John Macquarrie, *In Search of Deity: An Essay in Dialectical Theism* (New York: Crossroad, 1985).

[17] On the latter option, see the analysis of Hans Frei's position in chapter 5.

also texts that lend themselves readily to meditative, even speculative readings.

Nor need the defense of Christian neo-Platonic readings of the scriptures be so general and indirect. For both Testaments also contain writings that can only be named meditative, often speculative, and sometimes even mystical: the Wisdom tradition of the Hebrew Scriptures, the meditative theology of manifestation of John, and the dialectical thought of Paul and the Pauline tradition. Even in terms of the common gospel, there is not one narrative, but four: the apocalyptic, interruptive, non-closure text of Mark; the salvation-history, identity-formation text of Luke-Acts; the community-formation, new Torah text of Matthew; and the meditative narrative of John. It is little wonder that the early patristic writers turned most frequently to John and parts of "Paul" (especially Colossians and Ephesians) to inaugurate their neo-Platonic mystical and speculative readings of Christian existence. For however strained Gregory of Nyssa's reading of Moses in the apophatic dark cloud of unknowing in the Book of Exodus may be, he was surely correct to find his "image" theology, and his Trinitarian reflections and even his apophatic inclinations in the great "mystical" readings of the common gospel narrative by John and "Paul." For the neo-Platonists, Christ as Logos is in the very self-expression, the identical image of God. Human being, in Christ, is, in its essence, an *imago Dei* and Christian life is a life *ad imaginem Dei*. For the love uniting the Father (Source) and Logos, manifests Godself in the very love that, as both *agape* (pure gift) and *eros*, should define the heart of the Christian spiritual life, both personal and communal.

The core of the neo-Platonist reading of the Scriptures is not a mere imposition of Hellenistic Platonism upon Jewish-Christian prophetic texts. Rather as both the Wisdom tradition and the Johannine and Pauline traditions testify, a mystical reading of the Scriptures, if faithful to the heart of the matter, is fully appropriate. All the great strands of Christian mysticism, I believe, are grounded in legitimate readings of John and "Paul" and the Wisdom literature: the image mysticism of Gregory and Origen and

Irenaeus; the Trinitarian theology of Orthodoxy and the Western tradition of the Victorines and Ruysbroeck; the love-mysticism of Bernard of Clairvaux and the great Carmelites, John of the Cross and Teresa of Avila; the apophatic theologies of Pseudo-Dionysus, John Scotus Eriugena, and Meister Eckhart. Modernized remnants of these same traditions[18] can be found in the Trinitarian dialectics of Hegel, the dipolar God of Whitehead, and the apophatic meditations of Heidegger and Wittgenstein as well as the theologies of Rahner and Tillich.

The intellectual situation of the patristic and medieval neo-Platonists encouraged Platonic readings of the Christian scriptures. The Scriptures allow for those readings: hence the neo-Platonic appeal to the Logos of John, the "image" of Colossians and Ephesians. Hence their insistence on the Trinitarian reality of God as Source, Logos and Spirit and their ability (through the many medieval debates on the relative priority of "love" and "knowledge") to develop both love-mysticism (Bernard) and apophatic intellectualist mysticism (Eckhart). The neo-Platonic mystical theologians, more than more traditional theologians, have always realized how inadequate all our "names" for God are. They have not resisted, therefore, apophatic demands as long as those demands are grounded in the Christian communal spiritual experience of (1) Christ as Logos, as the Image of God, the Second "Person" of the Trinity, and (2) the Christian spiritual experience of love in the Christ as an experience of God's own self as Spirit — the Spirit who, as God, lovingly unites us to Father and Son even as the Spirit unites Father and Son to one another in God.

---

[18] See the illuminating studies of Hegel, Whitehead and Heidegger in John Macquarrie, *In Search of Deity*, pp. 125-139 (Hegel); pp. 139-153 (Whitehead); pp. 153-171 (Heidegger). On Wittgenstein and Buddhism here, see the contrasting views of Andrew P. Tuck, *Comparative Philosophy and the Philosophy of Scholarship*, pp. 28-30, 74-93; and Chris Gudmunsen, *Wittgenstein and Buddhism* (New York: Harper & Row, 1977). Hegel, Whitehead and even Heidegger have certain clear affinities to aspects of the great neo-Platonic traditions. Wittgenstein has affinities, if at all, only to the radically apophatic side of the tradition: which is perhaps the reason for recent debates on Wittgenstein and Buddhism.

However theologically defensible the neo-Platonic Christian tradition is (even on emanation as *one* way to interpret creation)[19] on inner-Christian, indeed scriptural terms, it is also, of course, true that it is just as dependent on the Greco-Roman culture within which such Christian speculative thought emerged. In that intellectual context, it is hardly surprising that the Logos and the *imago dei* should prove so central to the tradition — even if the extraordinary developments of the Trinitarian, love, and apophatic strands of the diverse Christian neo-Platonists are genuinely distinct and sometimes conflicting developments beyond the original Logos tradition.

This Greco-Roman cultural and intellectual background makes all the more intriguing the thought that if Christian theological speculation occurred in an East Asian cultural and intellectual context, a radically kenotic theology indeed rather than an image-theology may well have developed.[20]

In the meantime, the clearest analogue in the Christian tradition to the Buddhist position may be found not in the image, Trinitarian, and love strands of the Christian neo-Platonists but in the radically apophatic strands culminating in the intellectualist and spiritual journey of Meister Eckhart. As several Buddhist and Christian thinkers, including Abe, have acknowledged, Eckhart remains the clearest Christian *analogue* to Buddhist thought. Hence a brief recall of the terms of the debate between Eckhart and Ruysbroeck may help to illuminate my own Christian theological differences from Buddhism.

The complexities of Eckhart's position continue to puzzle interpreters. Indeed, the complexities are such that Rudolph Otto

[19] See the essays in David Burrell and Bernard McGinn, eds., *God and Creation: An Ecumenical Symposium* (Notre Dame, IN: University of Notre Dame Press, 1990).

[20] See here the important essay of Masao Abe, "Kenotic God and Dynamic Sunyata," in John B. Cobb, Jr. and Christopher Ives, eds., *The Emptying God: A Buddhist-Jewish-Christian Conversation* (Maryknoll: Orbis, 1990) pp. 3-69. I have adapted a section of my own response to Abe in that volume for the present study: the much longer essay on Abe is entitled, "Kenosis, Sunyata and Trinity: A Dialogue with Masao Abe," pp. 135-57.

could compare Eckhart to Shankara while D. T. Suzuki found the more apt comparision to be Nāgārjuna.[21] There remains, as well, continuing debates over the accuracy of the posthumous papal condemnation of some propositions of Eckhart in the bull *In Agro Dominico.* Moreover, in philosophy and in Christian theology, the more radical recent readings of Eckhart tend to compare his position to the more radical — that is, apophatic — side of Heidegger (Caputo and Schurmann) while other interpreters (McGinn and Colledge) argue for the importance not only of the more apophatic of the vernacular sermons but also of the scholastic categories of the more systematic Latin works.[22]

I cannot presume to resolve the difficulties of the expert interpreters. Fortunately, for the present limited purposes, that is unnecessary. Rather, informed by my own reading of the relevant texts and some principal interpreters, I shall confine my comments on Eckhart to two principal questions relevant for the dialogue with Buddhism. The first issue may be called one of spirituality. What strikes a reader most about Eckhart's texts (as indeed of most Buddhism) is a spirituality (or religious awareness) that is marked, above all, by two characteristics: intellectualism and radical detachment. Here a rigorous intellectualism not only is not divorced from the spirituality but is a central element

[21] See Rudolf Otto, *Mysticism East and West: Shankara and Meister Eckhart* (New York: Macmillan, 1932); Daisetz Teitaro Suzuki, *Mysticism: Christian and Buddhist* (New York: Harper & Bros., 1957).

[22] Edmund Colledge, "Meister Eckhart: His Times and His Writings," *The Thomist* 42 (1978) 240-258; Colledge, "Historical Data," in Edmund Colledge, O.S.A., and Bernard McGinn, trs. and eds., *Meister Eckhart: The Essential Sermons, Commentaries, Treatises and Defense* (New York: Paulist, 1981) pp. 5-24; McGinn, "Theological Summary," ibid., pp. 24-62; McGinn, "The God Beyond God: Theology and Mysticism in the Thought of Meister Eckhart," *Journal of Religion* 61 (1981) 1-19; Vladimir Lossky, *Théologie négative et connaissance de Dieu chez Maître Eckhart* (Paris: Vrin, 1960); the commentaries of Reiner Schürmann in *Meister Eckhart: Mystic and Philosopher* (Bloomington: Indiana University Press, 1987); John D. Caputo, *The Mystical Element in Heidegger's Thought* (Athens, OH: Ohio University Press, 1978); Bernard McGinn, ed., *Meister Eckhart: Teacher and Preacher* (New York: Paulist, 1986), pp. 2-41.

in it. For Eckhart, this shows his fidelity to his Dominican tradition in contrast to the greater love orientation of Bernard of Clairvaux and the Franciscans. This intellectualism, in turn, leads to a spirituality, in Eckhart, of radical detachment that bears remarkable resemblances to the non-attachment, non-clinging spirituality of all forms of Buddhism. Like the Buddhists and unlike the love-mystics, Eckhart sometimes seems to accord a "higher" spiritual role to radical detachment than to Christian love. This causes serious consequences in his theology. On the one hand, unlike some, but by no means all, Christian mystics, Eckhart is not interested in such intense experiences as rapture or ecstasy but, like Zen Buddhists, far more interested in illuminating our true awareness of the everyday. In the Buddhist case, nirvana and samsara are one. In Eckhart's case, the disclosure of the Godhead beyond God is, at the same time, the disclosure of our release to the everyday life of activity-in-the-world. Eckhart's remarkable reading of the Martha-Mary story is especially illustrative here for, in his reading, it is the active-contemplative Martha and not (as for many Christian contemplatives) the purely contemplative Mary who is the best illustration of the Christian contemplative's life as a life-in-the-world "without a why."

These affinities (not *identities*) in the kind of spiritual awareness of Eckhart and Zen make plausible the appeal of Eckhart to Buddhist thinkers. This same kind of spirituality of radical detachment and intellectualism leads to some of the more radically apophatic conceptualities of Eckhart, especially his famous insistence on the "Godhead beyond God" wherein even the names Father, Son, and Spirit are deemed inappropriate. For Eckhart, "nothingness" receives an unusual radicality for a Christian thinker. To be sure, as Buddhist thinkers have been quick to note, even Eckhart's "nothingness" is not the "absolute nothingness" of Zen thought.

That this is true can be seen in the fact that, however radically apophatic Eckhart is for a Christian thinker, he remains a God-obsessed thinker who constantly shifts, in different contexts, his language of transcendentals for both God and the Godhead beyond God. Not only Nothingness but One, Intelligence, and *Esse* seem to him appropriate if always inadequate language. Whether all Eckhart's language can be rendered coherent without either loss of all *Christian* God-language or without reducing his position to some more familiar Christian understanding of God remains the principal question still under dispute, despite *In Agro Dominico*. What is relatively clear, however, especially but not solely in the Latin texts, as McGinn argues, is Eckhart's unique use of the languages of predication, analogy, and dialectic.[23]

The dialectical language of Eckhart bears some striking resemblances to much Buddhist use of dialectics. In Eckhart's case, all his dialectical language for the Godhead and God can occur only after the possibilities and limits of predication and analogy have been tried. What is striking, for example, about Eckhart's use of analogy is its difference from his Dominican forebear, Thomas Aquinas. For Eckhart, however faithful to Thomas' language of analogy, exactly reverses its meaning: only God can provide the proper analogy. Indeed, this is true for Eckhart to the point where we are left with "extrinsic" attribution language rather than either Thomist "intrinsic" attribution or "proportionality."

Lest one think that Eckhart is an early proponent of Barth's *analogia fidei* against *analogia entis* one must note that this "failure" of traditional analogical language (and, before it, of traditional predication) becomes, for Eckhart, an occasion to note the need for a radically dialectical language. Here, as McGinn shows, is where Eckhart makes his most original moves — for the Godhead as One is indistinct and precisely as such is distinct from all reality (and vice versa). In more familiar terms, precisely the divine transcendence of all reality renders the divine reality immanent to all reality (and vice versa). This radically

---

[23] See the illuminating article by Bernard McGinn, "Meister Eckhart on God as Absolute Unity," in Dominic O'Meara, ed., *Neoplatonism and Christian Thought* (Albany: State University of New York Press, 1982), pp. 128-39. I follow McGinn's (and Lossky's) interpretation on dialectic in Eckhart.

dialectical understanding of indistinction and distinction, of immanence and transcendence, allows Eckhart to interpret both the *bullitio* of the emergence of the divine relations of the Trinity and, in creation, the *ebullitio* of the birth of the Word in the soul. In the return spiritual-intellectual journey, the soul returns to the Trinity and, in a final negation of radical apophatic detachment and radically apophatic dialectical thought, even breaks through to the Godhead beyond God. Thus can Eckhart, in a final paradox, *pray* to God to free him *from* God.

Even in the abbreviated form given above, one cannot but find Eckhart's intellectual-spiritual journey a remarkable one for a Christian. He can even be said to go a long way — although not all the way — with a Buddhist. But Eckhart's dialectic nonetheless demands a move which Buddhism does not; the self-manifestation of the Godhead in the distinct *bullitio* as the Trinity and the *ebullitio* of the creature. To be more exact, a Buddhist dialectic of dynamic sunyata may have a similar self-manifestation character insofar as dynamic sunyata manifests itself *as* wisdom and *as* compassion to the enlightened one. But this is still unlike Eckhart's explicit revision of neo-Platonic "emanation" language into the more radically dialectical language of *bullitio* and *ebullitio* (and, allied to that, on the human side of awareness, the birth of the Word in the soul and the "breakthrough" of the soul to the Godhead).

In Buddhist terms, Eckhart's "Godhead beyond God" is a route to, but is not finally an awareness of, "absolute nothingness." In Eckhartian Christian terms, a Buddhist needs to show how *dialectically* "dynamic sunyata" is not only immanent in all and thereby transcendent (and vice versa) but how that immanence-transcendence discloses itself as wisdom and as compassion. Here Christian neo-Platonism, especially in its more intellectualist, detached, and apophatic expressions, may have much to suggest. For, as far as I can see, the Buddhist needs to know why dynamic sunyata is necessarily disclosed *as* wise and *as* compassionate.

But this "Eckhartian" criticism is not my central point. For, impelled by the Buddhist-Christian dialogue to rethink Eckhart, I nevertheless remain puzzled whether the Christian understanding of God can receive as radically an apophatic character as Eckhart sometimes insists upon. I say this not to doubt the greater need to recover the apophatic tradition in Christian theology nor to doubt that no-thingness needs to be thought seriously in that tradition in relationship to such traditional (but difficult!) language as One, Intelligence, Being, or Creativity.

It is possible (I suspect, but do not yet know) that Eckhart's "Godhead beyond God" language may be appropriate Christian theological language — not merely in the relatively easy sense of one way to acknowledge the radical inadequacy of all our God-language, but in the more difficult dialectical sense of a more adequate naming of what Christians call God. For that reason, at this time and prior to further reflection impelled by the Buddhist-Christian dialogue and the rethinking of the apophatic tradition, I find myself, in Christian theological terms, more with Jan Ruysbroeck than with Meister Eckhart.[24] To continue the parallel with Eckhart, one may furnish the Christian theological reasons to move in Ruysbroeck's direction for understanding the Christian God in terms of both spirituality and theology. In the Christian spiritual life (here Merton in his famous dialogue with Suzuki clearly agrees with Ruysbroeck), the move to radical negation and nothingness is construed by the Christian as one important moment of awareness in the larger sphere of awareness of the fuller Christian life. Even Eckhart, with his language of *bullitio* and *ebullitio* may agree here.

In the Christian construal, the most radical negations of the cloud of unknowing and the acknowledgment of nothingness must, through its own power of awareness, yield to the self-manifestation (emanation, *bullitio-ebullitio*, revelation) of the Divine Reality (whether named Godhead or God).

Theologically, this means, as Ruysbroeck clearly sees, that the

---

[24] See Louis Dupré, *The Common Life*. Dupré makes clear his indebtedness here to the great tradition of Flemish scholarship on Ruysbroeck.

radical indistinction, the no-thingness of Eckhart's Godhead-beyond God, will necessarily manifest itself in the Christian life as the self-manifesting Father-Son-Spirit. Where Eckhart is unclear in his language about applying his diverse transcendental terms (One, *Esse*, Intelligence), sometimes to the Godhead and sometimes to the Father-Source, Ruysbroeck is clear. In Christian terms, all our language for God is inadequate. The radical negations of the spiritual life demand radical negations of all our names for God. Yet the Christian experience and thereby awareness of God's wisdom in the Logos and God's love in the Spirit remain our central clues to the reality we hesitantly name God. Insofar as Christians experience Godself as Source, Logos, and Spirit they find their central insight into God's own reality as always self-manifesting. That self-manifestation of the Father as Logos-Image is the Son. That relationship of divine self-manifestation is the Spirit. Christians find these conceptualities for understanding the divine reality through their very experiences and awareness of wisdom and love. Those clues to the source, order, and end of all reality allow them to name God as an always self-manifesting God — as Father-Son-Spirit (or Mother-Daughter-Spirit or Source-Logos-Spirit).[25]

In traditional theological terms, the "economic" Trinity is our main clue to the "ontological" Trinity of God's own reality. Nor need one fear that there will always be a "fourth" — the divine essence in all Christian Trinitarian understanding of God — insofar as one grasps, as Ruysbroeck clearly does, that God's essence *is* dialectically self-manifesting and thereby is necessarily Father-Son-Spirit.

I believe, furthermore, that Macquarrie[26] (and Hegel and the

---

[25] I see no good theological reason to resist the use of both male and female imagery for language for God. Feminist theology, with its emphasis on relationality, seems (as several feminist theologians insist) intrinsically open to a Trinitarian understanding of God. On the issue of language for God here, see Sallie McFague, *Models of God: Theology for an Ecological, Nuclear Age* (Philadelphia: Fortress, 1987).

[26] Macquarrie, *In Search of Deity*, pp. 3-59; 199-212.

entire neo-Platonic tradition before him) is correct to state that this Christian insight implies that "natural theology" should also feel obliged to show the intrinsically incarnational and relational Trinitarian structure of all reality. Unlike not only the Barthians but also the Thomists (with their distinction between "natural" mysteries and "supernatural" mysteries), the neo-Platonists (including, here, Hegelians and some Whiteheadians, Rahnerians, and Tillichians) develop philosophical positions that attempt to show, minimally, the reasonableness (and not merely the Thomist non-contradiction) of an incarnational, relational, and Trinitarian understanding of all reality. Such an enterprise, to be sure, demands a full incarnational metaphysics of relationality, which may or may not cohere with Buddhist metaphysics. That is clearly another discussion for another time and place.

In the meantime, the Christian Trinitarian (self-manifesting, radically relational) understanding of the Divine Reality so well expressed by Ruysbroeck may suggest that Buddhists too may find such understanding suggestive for their very distinct enterprise. For insofar as Buddhist thought is dependent on Buddhist practice and spiritual awareness, then the Buddhist awareness of sunyata as wise and compassionate may suggest the need to develop a transcendent-immanent dialectic further into a dialectic of sunyata as ultimate source-wisdom-compassion.

Clearly, even if this suggestion were agreed to, the Buddhist and the Christian would still not be saying the same thing. But the radically relational and self-manifesting *structure* of Ultimate Reality would be commonly affirmed. And that would render further conversation on such distinct issues as the "duality" of God and all creatures (in the Buddhist critique of Christianity) and the coherence of radical relationality and radically autonomous "suchness" and its puzzling "freedom" and "nonfreedom" (in the Christian critique of Buddhism) more intelligible — or at least, more discussable in mutually intelligible terms.

To find such terms is the first step needed in this great new dialogue of our day. We cannot finally stay with the Buddhist. As I suggest above, I do not believe that we can even finally stay with Meister Eckhart. But only those who have allowed the challenge of the otherness of Eckhart to be real — like Ruysbroeck and Cusanus — are likely to lead us further in the kind of theological retrieval now needed. Similarly, only those Christians in an emerging world church in a polycentric global culture, who are willing to listen to the challenge of the otherness of the Buddhist way can move us further along the route that we all need to take: a mystico-prophetic journey where the inter-religious dialogue will become an integral part of all Christian theological thought. Clearly the Buddhist and the Christian are not the same way. But neither are we two, in any easy way, merely other to one another. Perhaps, as the Buddhists suggest, we are neither the same nor other, but not-two. Only the further dialogue will tell.

DIALOGUE AND THE PROPHETIC-MYSTICAL OPTION

Christian Theology and Dialogue

As the preceding reflections indicate, dialogue among the religions is no longer a luxury but a theological necessity. The praxis of dialogue demands primacy before any rush to theoretical revisions within theology. To be sure, true theory is also grounded in praxis — the praxis of critical reflection. Still the move to any serious theological revision open to the demands of religious pluralism suggests a need to be wary of theoretical reflections not grounded in both the demanding praxis of the kind of critical reflection proper to all theory and the transformative praxis of inter-religious dialogue where the "other" becomes not a projected but a genuine other.

Theoretical reflection on dialogue itself, moreover, suggests that only where the subject-matter and not the subject's consciousness is allowed to take over does true dialogue happen. Every subject inevitably enters that unnerving place, the dialogue, with certain expectations on what the relevant questions are and who the other may be. It cannot be overemphasized that, if genuine dialogue is to occur, we must be willing to put everything at risk. Otherwise, we do not allow attention to the logic of questioning elicited by this particular subject matter (however different or other — even, at times, terrifyingly other, as Levinas correctly insists). For my part I cannot but enter an inter-religious dialogue as other than a Christian. Even my willingness to enter is, for me, a result of a two-fold commitment: a faith commitment to love of God and neighbor — the heart of Christianity in that command and empowerment of the God decisively manifested in Jesus Christ; and an ethical commitment to these honorable (Western) meanings of what genuine dialogue is (from Plato to Gadamer).

A Western ethical commitment to what reason-as-dialogue and

my Christian commitment to the ethical-religious praxis of inter-
religious dialogue as one of the "works-of-love" may unite to
impel one to enter that *fascinans et tremendum* place, the pluralistic and ambiguous dialogue among the religions in our day. For
many of us, our prior theological self-understanding as modern
Christians had already occasioned an abandonment of any purely
"exclusivist" understanding of the revelation of Jesus Christ. For
some (myself included) one or another liberal version of Christian
"inclusivism" and "finality" once seemed adequate to the pluralistic situation as well as appropriate to a revised understanding of
the tradition. Liberal inclusivism seemed adequate insofar as it
provided one honest Christian way to affirm other revelations
and ways of salvation as real ways. Theological inclusivism
seemed appropriately Christian by providing a theological
account of how these other ways could be included, in principle,
either as constituted by or normatively judged by the Christian
belief in general revelation and the universal salvific will of the
God disclosed with finality in Jesus Christ.

But the liberal inclusivist ways, too, I now realize, must also be
put at risk in the new inter-religious dialogues.[1] The new question
is to find a way to formulate a Christian theological question on
religious pluralism in such manner that a genuinely new answer
may be forthcoming without abandoning Christian identity. The
"answer" is unlikely to be, as some suggest, by shifting from a
"christocentric" to a "theocentric" position. This Christian response seems more a postponement of the issue rather than an
adequate response to it. For insofar as Christians know the God

---

[1] To state this more exactly: the Christian theological move from exclusivism
to inclusivism is one of the enduring accomplishments of liberal Christian
theology; the question of models of "inclusivism" and the possible adequacy or
inadequacy of such models for christology in the inter-religious dialogue remains,
in my judgment, an open question. For some examples of Christian theologians
who have abandoned any earlier model of inclusivism see the essays in John Hick
and Paul Knitter, eds., *The Myth of Christian Uniqueness* (New York: Orbis,
1987). See, as well, the review of three of these options (Hick, Kaufman, Ruether)
by Schubert Ogden in his essay, "Problems in the Case for a Pluralistic Theology
of Religions," *Journal of Religion* 68 (1988) 483-508.

(as pure, unbounded Love) that all Christian models of theocentrism demand, they know *that* God in and through the decisive revelation of God in Jesus Christ. Correlatively, insofar as Christians are willing to enter dialogue they are thus willing either because of their prior ethical commitment to reason-as-dialogical or, more likely, their Christian understanding of *Christian* faith-working-through-love as now demanding inter-religious dialogue (that new work of love).

Like many others I now find myself in the uncharted territory of the new inter-religious dialogue aware that both our present situation demands that entry and, as suggested above, so does Christian faith. Is it possible to have an adequate theological response to the full implications of inter-religious dialogue for Christian theological self-understanding yet?

For some, the answer is yes. For myself, I have no such confidence at present. That we should examine critically all prior Christian theological answers in the light of the interreligious dialogue I do not doubt. That we should risk articulating new Christian theological answers (like the move past "christocentrism" to "theocentrism") I also do not doubt. Yet if we have good reason to think that "theocentrism" simply recalls the issue of "christocentrism" by another name, then we may need to ask more questions in actual dialogues with others and ourselves before announcing a new christology or a new theocentrism. It is, in fact, more exact to speak of two crucial and related dialogues: first, the interreligious dialogue which provides the principal new religious praxis which is transforming all of us and which gives rise to new theological thoughts and theories; and second, the inner-Christian dialogue, where Christian theologians attempt to report to others what possibilities they now foresee.

As these essays may serve to suggest, my own attempts at the first form of interreligious dialogue have been serious but modest: with Jews; with Buddhists; with the archaic or primal religions through the work of Mircea Eliade and other colleagues, especially in history of religions; and, in a strange way unnecessary to spell out here, with new work in ancient Greek religion — and not only ancient Greek philosophy. I hope that each of those dialogues as well as other needed dialogues will increase over the years. The praxis of interreligious dialogue itself, I believe, does not merely bear a "religious dimension." It *is* a religious experience: hence, the "mutational person" demands of Raimondo Pannikar and other Christians makes far more sense to me now than ever before.[2]

Each dialogue is likely to make it possible to revise aspects of the tradition which need revision and to discover other forgotten, indeed often repressed, aspects of the great tradition. Some examples: the post-Holocaust Jewish-Christian dialogue has provoked, for me, a greater realization not only of the irretrievably Judaic (and especially prophetic-eschatological) character of Christianity. That crucial dialogue has also made me more aware of needed revisions in christology (as in the language I now employ of the always-already, not yet Christ), while also making me aware of the revolting underside of christology in the history of Christian anti-Semitism. The work of Jewish theologians has also occasioned a needed Christian theological reappropriation of the other *tremendum* aspects of the covenantal God.[3] Indeed, many Christian formulations of God as love begin to seem, at best, unfinished — as *Lamentations* and much of the Wisdom literature suggests, as Luther's *deus nudus* insisted, as Barth's attempted recovery of the "wrath of God" suggests, and as post-Holocaust Jewish theology suggests with even greater force.

Moreover, the primal religions (too often ignored in theological interreligious dialogue) occasion further reflection on the primal (or manifestory) character of both Christianity and Judaism. Minimally, primal manifestation should be the necessary dialecti-

[2] Christian theology, in its origins, is profoundly influenced by Greek philosophy. It is, at the least, an interesting thought-experiment to consider, as well, ancient (pre-classical, classical and Hellenistic) Greek religions more fully for Christian theological self-understanding as intrinsically dialogical. On Greek religion, see Walter Burkert, *Greek Religion* (Cambridge, MA: Harvard University Press, 1985).

[3] For an example of Pannikar's important work, see *The Intrareligious Dialogue* (New York: Paulist, 1978).

cal counterpart to the more familiar prophetic and proclamation trajectories — as the prophetically oriented Latin American liberation theologians who are presently rethinking "popular religion" see. A rethinking of the ancient Greek religions (including pre-classical goddess religions) have occasioned, for me, new reflections on the diversity of resources in the Greek side of our heritage. That diversity historically has been often violently suppressed by the early Christian theological decision to follow Plato (rather than, say, Sappho or Hesiod or Herodotus or Aeschylus) in the reading of classical Greek and pre-classical (e.g., goddess) religion. Finally, the Buddhist-Christian dialogue is the place where, at least for myself, the full terror of otherness has been most acute. The Buddhist-Christian dialogue can occasion, it is true, a new appreciation (as in John Cobb's work) of the possibilities of "mutual transformation" in dialogue with traditions like Amida Buddhism and the Boddhisattva traditions. It can also occasion the discovery of aspects of the Christian tradition like the radically apophatic traditions as well as thoughts on the fuller implications of a "kenotic christology."

Yet that same Buddhist-Christian dialogue, especially when it turns to Zen Buddhism, seems to call all sanguine language of commonality and complementarity into very serious question. I am not aware of *any* strand of Christianity, however forgotten or repressed, that answers the profoundly religious question of transience as the Buddhist does. Is the Buddhist simply wrong? Or is the Buddhist way a disclosure of another "way" (for the Christian, therefore, some revelation and salvation) not previously glimpsed in the Christian way — but open to, challenging to, transformative of our way? How, if at all, we might be able to include so different an other as the Buddhist only further dialogical praxis will be able one day to suggest. Then and only then will we begin to know how such Buddhist praxis may relate to Christian soteriology and thereby to any christological claim. It is true that Buddhist notions of Ultimate Reality as emptiness do help to break any dualism in Christian notions of God and creation. Yet, for the Christian and Jew, some duality (not dualism) between Creator and creation will always be affirmed. Buddhists can also force Christian theologians to realize that theism can be a subtle way to "cling" and not let go to God. As suggested earlier, Buddhists can occasion for Christians a rediscovery of the insights of Eckhart. Yet, however radical Eckhart's language of the Godhead-beyond-God for Christian self-understanding is, even that is not Nāgārjuna's view of either language or Ultimate Reality. They are and remain radically different.

It is true, as John Hick argues, that all great traditions seem to occasion a radical turn from self-centeredness to Reality-centeredness.[4] Yet the differences at every step in these different turns — of the understandings of self, salvation-enlightenment, and Ultimate Reality — seem so striking, so different and other, that all I really know is that I do not know (and that with a relatively *indocta ignorantia*). With such differences as these how can a plausible generalization — on either commonality or complementarity or dialectical relationships or sheer difference — be made? The future may tell, but the present, as far as I can see, provides many hints and guesses but no adequate Christian theological answer. Perhaps another generation or two of thinkers who take the interreligious dialogue for granted as a necessary religious and intellectual praxis for all serious religious thinkers in our day is needed before any adequate response is possible. In the meantime, we should all try to articulate some tentative suggestions for change.

The Mystico-Prophetic Trajectories of the Religions

In all the major religious traditions, there is a search for new ways to unite those mystical and prophetic trajectories we saw in the first essay. In the major Western monotheistic traditions of Judaism, Christianity, and Islam the debates are particularly

---

[4] For Hick's most extended analysis, see *An Interpretation of Religion: Human Responses to the Transcendent* (New Haven: Yale University Press, 1989); for an analysis of Hick's work, see Chester Gillis, *A Question of Final Belief: John Hick's Pluralistic Theory of Salvation* (London: Macmillan, 1989).

intense. Recall the continuing conflict in the Islamic traditions on the relationship of Sufi mysticism to the prophetic case of Islam. Note the debates in Jewish theology occasioned by the pioneering work of Gershom Scholem on Kabbalah, to find a less than marginal place in Judaism for the outbursts of the mystical and, simultaneously, the return of the archaic in the classic expressions of Kabbalistic mysticism. There are many analogous discussions in Christian theology centered around the need to rethink the relationships of the contemplative traditions to the action-oriented political, liberation, and feminist theologies. There are the new discussions of "popular religion" among the Latin American liberation theologians. In the United States the analysis of the primal African roots in the mystico-political rhythms of African-American gospel, spiritual, and blues music as appropriated by African-American liberation theologians sound the same mystico-political note.[5] Many feminist theologians, meanwhile, are recovering the archaic goddess traditions, the Wisdom Sophia tradition, and the language and practices of women mystics to unite these more mystical-oriented trajectories to the fundamentally prophetic ethical-political orientations of most feminist theology.

At the same time, some thinkers in the great Eastern traditions, so at home in more mystical orientations, have been incorporating more social-ethical and political-prophetic perspectives into their own thought and practices. The influence of Gandhi on neo-Hindu thought is merely the clearest example among many of this modern drive. In modern Japanese Buddhism, both Zen and Pure Land, the rethinking of how Buddhist compassion should relate to justice (e.g., justice, not only compassion, for the non-indigenous Ainu people in Japan) demonstrates the same kind of development. Moreover, as Hinduism, Sikhism, and Buddhism in their many forms have become live options for Westerners this already prominent tendency is likely to increase. The attempt to unite the mystical and the ethical-political, moreover, is illustra-

[5] For example, see the analyses of James Cone, *The Spirituals and the Blues* (New York: Harper & Row, 1972).

ted well by the exceptional, self-transcending individuals in the different traditions: as classically in Gandhi's neo-Hindu rereading of Tolstoy's interpretation of Christianity; and, reciprocally, Martin Luther King, Junior's Christian reading of Gandhi. The future is, however, unlikely to be confined to such exceptional individuals. The Buddhist case is especially illustrative here: as Buddhism has become a Western religion, the shifts in Buddhist self-understanding to a more mystico-political one is as striking as the earlier shifts in classic Buddhism as it moved past its own Indian origins to Southeast Asia to Tibet to China to Japan and now to the West.

The resurgent interest among philosophers and theologians in neo-Confucianism is also illustrative of these new mystico-political orientations. Neo-Confucianism has been exceptionally successful in its ability to unite the civic and political concerns of classical Confucianism with the more mystical orientations of classical Taoism and Chan Buddhism.[6] The internal debates on how to unite the mystical and the prophetic within each religion, moreover, are complicated by one of the outstanding facts of late twentieth century religious life: the increasing impact of the interreligious dialogue (and thus the challenge of "other" alternatives) for each tradition's own self-understanding. I have, throughout these essays, tried to indicate some features of that impact for Christian theological self-understanding.

Indeed, this drive to a mystico-prophetic reading has been the principal motive of the present essays. The first essay — an appropriately tentative genre here — argued how the mystical and prophetic categories of religious thought, rhetorically construed, help to illuminate the differences between Lacan's postmodern ("mystical") reading of the great modern "prophetic"

---

[6] For example, here see Judith A. Berling, *The Syncretic Religion of Lin Chao-en* (New York: Columbia University Press, 1980); William de Bary and the Conference on Seventeenth Century Chinese Thought, *The Unfolding of Neo-Confucianism* (New York: Columbia University Press, 1976); Julia Ching, *To Acquire Wisdom: The Way of Wang Yang-Ming* (New York: Columbia University Press, 1976).

texts of Freud. The second essay, by rethinking and revising William James, developed some general philosophical and religious criteria as heuristic guides to philosophical and implicitly theological assessments of interreligious dialogue. Indeed these more general philosophical criteria were developed, to be sure, with Christian theological concerns in mind. The hermeneutic emphasis on manifestation and disclosure has genuine affinities with the mystical orientations and their emphasis on revelation or enlightenment. At the same time, the pragmatic ethical-political criteria have clear affinities to the prophetic emphasis on salvation as demanding both justice and love.

The next two essays moved in a more explicitly Christian theological direction in order to highlight the two major forms of mystically-oriented "otherness" needing hermeneutical and theological attention. Hence the analysis of Mircea Eliade's hermeneutics of the archaic other as an occasion to reassess the great primal locative traditions. Theologically construed, moreover, Eliade's hermeneutics also bears remarkable resemblances to the manifestation and cosmic-mystical orientation of Eastern Christianity. Just as Eliade's great hermeneutic of the archaic shows its affinities to the Romantics' interest in India and the archaic archetypes as well as the great literary modernists' love for "disclosure" and "epiphany," so too the revival of interest by many Western Christian theologians in Buddhism bears strong affinities with much post-modern thought. The last two essays, therefore, have emphasized those aspects of the contemporary inter-religious dialogue that highlight the need to retrieve the classical Christian mystical traditions — either through the recovery of the archaic traditions, the many traditions of Hinduism, or the various Buddhist traditions.

I remain convinced that one signal opportunity for Christian theology as a result of serious religious dialogue is the retrieval of the great Christian mystical traditions: the image tradition of Gregory of Nyssa and Origen and their development of a cosmic Christianity; the Trinitarian mysticism of the Cappadocians and Augustine and, above all, Ruysbroec; and the great love mysticism tradition of the classic Cistercians and Bernard of Clairvaux to the great Spanish Carmelites, Teresa of Avila and John of the Cross.

But it is also clearly time to try to restore the balance of these essays away from their almost exclusive emphasis on retrieving the mystical traditions. Hence, in this final reflection, I shall concentrate on the present need to recover the central prophetic core of Christianity in the context of the interreligious dialogue. Here the need is for any prophetic tradition (even one rethought as prophetic-mystical) to establish, beyond the "no-self" of Buddhism and the "death of the subject" of post-modern thought alike, a Christian agent with enough freedom to allow for a commitment to the prophetic struggle for justice. The Christian agent, as we shall see, is also the prophetic agent of the Bible.

Narrative and the Interpretation of Christianity

Most religions have sacred stories or narratives that play an important role for that community's identity. Among religious communities whose sacred stories have become canonical "scripture," the Christian emphasis on narrative seems unique. Even in contrast to rabbinic Judaism, Christianity seems peculiar: both communities share one collection of sacred stories (the Hebrew Bible, the Christian Old Testament). The Jewish community, moreover, has developed a series of brilliant commentaries on the biblical stories that have played almost as large a role for community self-identity as the biblical texts themselves.[7] The role of *haggadah* in Rabbinic Judaism from the first century C.E. to today makes clear how important both the biblical narratives and the later rabbinic stories are for Jewish self-identity. Yet, except for some revisionary interpretations of Judaism (e.g., Martin Buber's)[8], the role of narrative *haggadah*, although prominent,

---

[7] Meir Sternberg, *The Poetics of Biblical Narrative* (Bloomington, IN: Indiana University Press, 1987); Michael Fishbane, *Biblical Interpretation in Ancient Israel* (Oxford: Clarendon, 1984).

[8] On Buber's unique use of narrative, see the forthcoming study by Steven Kepnes.

does not replace the role of *hallakah* (or law and the commentaries on law). Even Reform Judaism does not shift the focus from *hallakah* to *haggadah* as distinct from revising the law, sometimes radically, in the light of modern conditions.

In Christianity, a similar story might be told with the category "doctrines" replacing "law."[9] By the late New Testament period, there are already "doctrines" (and laws). Christian theologians, even in the modern period, have spent a good deal of their time either clarifying, defending, or revising the classical "doctrines" for community self-understanding (recall Hegel, Schleiermacher, Bultmann, Rahner, Küng). In the last fifteen years, however, a curious sea-change seems to have occurred. Christian theologians have begun to emphasize that the New Testament is focused not on "doctrine" (which is a relatively late genre) but on narrative — more exactly, "gospel." Might not this "genre-choice" of gospel as proclaiming narrative have implications for Christian self-understanding? What is both fascinating and confusing about the present discussion of narrative in Christian theology is how the debate seems to cut across the usual ideological divisions. Political theologians like the German political theologian Johann Baptist Metz, the feminist theologian Elizabeth Schüssler-Fiorenza, the African-American theologian James Cone, the Latin American liberation theologian Gustavo Gutierrez, as well as many more conservative theologians: all, in distinct and sometimes conflicting ways, highlight the importance of narrative for Christian self-understanding. The liberation theologians, for example, insist that Christians should read the "passion narratives" in the light of the liberation narrative of Exodus (and vice versa). Feminist theologians, like Schüssler-Fiorenza in her important exegetical work, *In Memory of Her*,[10] insist that the original New Testament narratives (which, she shows, highlight

---

[9] For analysis of the genre "doctrine," see George Lindbeck, *The Nature of Doctrine: Religion and Theology in a Post-Liberal Age* (Philadelphia: Westminster, 1984); Alister E. McGrath, *The Genesis of Doctrine* (Oxford: Blackwell, 1990).

[10] Elisabeth Schüssler-Fiorenza, *In Memory of Her: A Feminist Theological Reconstruction of Christian Origins* (New York: Crossroad, 1983).

the role of women far more than later tradition chose to remember) must be reread as prior to the later, more patriarchal doctrines. The German political theologians (Metz and Moltmann) tend both to make more general philosophical claims for narrative (like Paul Ricoeur) and to insist that those philosophical claims are theologically determined by the overriding centrality of the passion narrative (more exactly, for Metz, the passion narrative as in the "interruptive" narrative of the memory of suffering).[11]

The same kinds of examples could easily be provided for both conservative and liberal theologians. Amidst all these proposals on the centrality of narrative for Christian identity lurk some disturbing questions. Some proposals seem like theological correlates to familiar philosophical proposals (e.g., Paul Ricoeur or Alastair MacIntyre)[12] by insisting that any individual and any community, as temporal and historical, can only understand itself in and through narrative. Insofar as we are creatures of temporality, we are forced to admit our historicity and thereby render our self-understanding in narrative terms. If one wants to describe Christianity (as distinct from presuming to "explain" it through the use of some more general theory), then the best way to do so is to provide a "thick description" by retelling the story. The describer should start with the "foundation story" of Jesus of Nazareth proclaimed by Christians to have lived and died in a particular place and time even as this Jesus Christ is affirmed as present ("risen") in the present Christian community.

Indeed, a generic approach to narrative is implicit in many Christian theological appeals to narrative. The disadvantage (or advantage?) of such "general narrativity" approaches (like Ricoeur's) to Christian narrative-identity is that the peculiarity of the *Christian* narrative may be lost in a legitimate concern to

[11] John Baptist Metz, *Faith in History and Society* (New York: Crossroad, 1980).

[12] Alasdair MacIntyre, *After Virtue: A Study in Moral Theory* (Notre Dame, IN: University of Notre Dame Press, 1981); Paul Ricoeur, *Time and Narrative*. 3 vols. (Chicago: University of Chicago Press, 1984-88); David Carr, *Time, Narrative and History* (Bloomington, IN: Indiana University Press, 1986).

show how the Christian narrative relates to (or merely instances?) more general human narratives — like religious narratives of human recalcitrance and fate's inevitability yielding "betrayal-narratives."[13] For "comparative" purposes such general narrative approaches to Christianity seem fruitful but limited. For one may wonder whether the Christian specificity is fully enough rendered in its particularity if brought too quickly under the two rubrics of a more general notion of "narrativity" and a more general notion of "religion".

Other theologians suggest that these more philosophically and comparatively oriented "narrative" readings of Christian identity are, indeed, too general to be of much help to the specifics of the Christian narrative.[14] Three more theological considerations prompt these later Christian narrativists. First, if the central Christian confession is "Jesus is the Christ," then one must tell the story of this particular Jesus in all its particularity in order to understand the confession itself.[15]

Second, narrative is the first and preferred mode of confession (or proclamation) used by the early Christian communities who wrote the New Testament texts in the genre of gospel, that genre of confessing narrative. To describe Christianity demands careful attention especially to the "passion-narratives" of the gospels. The third consideration is less one on how to read the first-century gospels in their own terms, than it is a modern story of the loss of a "narrative reading" by modern Christianity. The story (and it too is a story) is a complex and controverted one.

[13] In Ricoeur's case, his magisterial theory of narrativity and temporality does not disallow his careful hermeneutical attention to Jewish and Christian specificity: see, especially, his forthcoming book on biblical narrative and his *Essays on Biblical Interpretation*, ed., Lewis M. Mudge (Philadelphia: Fortress, 1980).

[14] For the debate, see the essays in Stanley Hauerwas and L. Gregory Jones, eds., *Why Narrative? Readings in Narrative Theology* (Grand Rapids, MI: Eerdmans, 1989).

[15] I have attended to this issue as well as my own assessment of the Frei-Lindbeck "narrativist" position in an essay entitled "On Reading the Scriptures Theologically" in the forthcoming Lindbeck Festschrift. On the confession, see Robert Grant with David Tracy, *A Short History of the Interpretation of the Bible* (Philadelphia: Fortress, 1984).

No one has told it more persuasively than Hans Frei in his influential book entitled *The Eclipse of Biblical Narrative*.[16] The story Frei relates, in its simplest plot, is this: with the emergence of historical consciousness in the eighteenth and nineteenth centuries, Christians (especially Protestant Christians in Britain and Germany) underwent a "great reversal" in their reading of the scriptures. In a pre-critical era, Christians (Calvin and Luther foremost among them) read the scriptures for their "plain sense," sometimes named the "literal sense." From the very beginning, Christian readers of the scriptures could allow for further kinds of reading as long as the plain sense of the narrative controlled the reading. For Frei, when the "literal sense" dominated (as, in different ways, it did for Thomas Aquinas or Luther), all was well. When some other mode of reading (e.g., the allegorical) took over, the "plain sense" of the narratives could be lost.[17] That "plain sense" of the Christian community read the gospel narratives as history-like and realistic.[18] Thus did Christians understand the identity of the main character, Jesus Christ, as rendered by the story. That rendering of the identity of Jesus Christ, moreover, allowed Christians to render their own true identity (both individually and communally) as disclosed by that

[16] Hans Frei, *The Eclipse of Biblical Narrative* (New Haven: Yale University Press, 1974). His constructive theological conclusions may be found in *The Identity of Jesus Christ* (Philadelphia: Fortress, 1975).

[17] The operative word is "could" not "must." Personally I remain persuaded (de Lubac, *et al.*) of the value of patristic and medieval allegorical readings. Surely the more "mystically-oriented" neo-Platonic theologians show this fruitfulness. The contemporary emphasis on "literal" readings, although clearly fruitful for the reasons cited in the text (and distinctly emphasized by Aquinas and Luther), seems both too narrow in focus and too peremptory in their discussions of "allegorical," or "mystical" or even "general hermeneutical" readings and concerns. For an example of the latter tendency, see Hans Frei, "The 'Literal Reading' of Biblical Narrative in the Christian Tradition: Does It Stretch or Will It Break?" in Frank McConnell, ed., *The Bible and Narrative Tradition* (New York: Oxford University Press, 1986), pp. 36-77.

[18] The "plain sense" means primarily how the Christian community traditionally read the scriptures (viz., as history-like and realistic). See the essay by Kathryn E. Tanner for a clarification of the uses of the term "plain sense" in "Theology and the Plain Sense," in Garrett Green, ed., *Scriptural Authority and Narrative Interpretation* (Philadelphia: Fortress, 1987).

narrative. The rest of reality was read through the biblical narrative and not vice versa.

With modernity, Frei's story continues, all this changed; a "great reversal" took place. Christians began to ask whether the "cognitive claims" of the biblical narrative were true on extra-biblical grounds (hence the emergence, with the deists, of a dominant interest in "revelation" as "knowledge"). Christians began to ask whether the historical events of the narrative were true by modern historical-critical criteria. In sum, the "plain sense" of the community ceased to provide Christians with their basic identity. For their Christian identity, Christians now had to go elsewhere. For the sense and the referent of the biblical narratives, once held together by the "plain sense" with which the community read them as realistic and history-like, were now split apart. The philosophers and theologians soon joined the historical-critical exegetes in demanding extra-biblical support for the narrative: either through historical-critical exegesis (as in the many "quests for the historical Jesus") or through philosophical or general cultural arguments.

In Frei's reading, therefore, the only hope of recovering Christian identity is to recover a "plain sense" reading of the biblical narratives again. For Frei, this demands abandoning the futile hope of "correlating" this narrative to some more general notions of "narrativity" or "religion" (or both).[19] This also demands reading the narratives more like literary critics read them (at least certain kinds of critics like Cleanth Brooks or Eric Auerbach).

As Frei's brilliant reading of Luke's gospel as rendering the identity of Jesus Christ for the Christian community in history-like and realistic fashion shows, there is a good deal to this so-called pure narrativist case.[20] As several desperate modern Christian attempts to replace the traditional Christian narrative with some alternative narrative while still claiming Christian identity

---

[19] Or, as noted in footnote 17, to any general hermeneutical theory. Also, see Gary Comstock, "Truth and Meaning: Ricoeur Versus Frei in Biblical Narrative," *Journal of Religion* 66 (1986) 117-140.

[20] Hans Frei, *The Identity of Jesus Christ*.

also demonstrate, there are also good reasons to find Frei's narrative on the "eclipse of biblical narrative" in modern Christianity illuminating. Frei's case is especially illuminating as a reading of Luke's gospel. But, unfortunately, for Frei's position and that of other pure narrativists, Luke is not the only gospel.[21] Indeed, only a "close reading" of all four gospels could test the claims of any particular narrative reading of Christianity. Consider the import of this issue for the questions of agency and freedom. How can we read the Christian narrative and defend the central place of freedom for an agent? How can we allow for a prophetic-mystical reading of the passion narratives?

The Prophetic Agent in Freedom: The Mystical-Prophetic Return to History

In the Christian theological tradition, the question of freedom has always been a central issue. The Christian interpretation of reality demands an agent who possesses authentic freedom. Since the time of Paul, the issue of the true freedom of the Christian can be interpreted summarily as the gift of freedom in Christ that both empowers and commands the agent to act responsibly before God and for others. Since the time of Augustine, this originally Pauline insight has been at the center of Western Christian self-interpretation.[22] One aspect of that Augustinian

---

[21] The difficulty is present not only for the meditative gospel of John and the un-realistic (indeed more modernist) Mark, but even for the genre-puzzling Gospel of Matthew. For an example of what seems to me to be a certain interpretive forcing of Frei's Lukan reading in the Gospel of Matthew, see the analyses of Matthew in Ronald Thiemann, *Revelation and Theology: The Gospel as Narrated Promise* (Notre Dame, IN: University of Notre Dame Press, 1985).

[22] The contrast of Augustine and pre-Augustinians on the gift of freedom made by Elaine Pagels and other scholars is, of course, sound. Her polemic against Augustine in the further issue of the dilemmas of the "self" seems to me as wrong-headed a critique as criticizing Freud's pessimism and tragic sensibility on the "psyche" for not sharing James' pre-Freudian optimism. Augustine deserves great criticism for much (including his polemical anti-Pelagian exaggerations in his later work). He does not deserve dismissal (any more than Freud does) for his extraordinary analysis of the dilemma of the self *curvatus in se*. For the other view, see Elaine Pagels, *Adam, Eve and the Serpent* (New York: Random House, 1989).

heritage has been developed by the Thomist tradition in Catholic theology ordinarily under the rubric of grace and freedom. The famous, if not notorious, debates on the relationships of grace and freedom in Thomas Aquinas have been fierce: the Banezian-Molinist dispute was merely the most famous of the series of impasses of those hermeneutical debates on Aquinas. In our own century, the creative interpretations of Maurice de la Taille (on "actuation"), Karl Rahner (on "quasi-formal causality") and Bernard Lonergan (on "contingent predication") are the most fruitful contemporary interpretations of Thomas Aquinas on this controverted issue.

The other side of the Augustinian heritage on grace and freedom has been most developed in the Reformation and in Catholic Jansenism. The classic *loci* here remain Luther's debate with Erasmus, especially Luther's *The Bondage of the Will* and his equally influential *The Freedom of the Christian*, as well as Calvin's reflections on predestination, and the reflections of Bishop Jansenius on Augustine and Pascal's Jansenist reflections. Those classic Christian debates have also been intense: from the Arminian debates among Calvinists to the revisionary understanding of the Hidden and Revealed God of Calvin and Luther to the continuing exegesis of both Jansenius and Pascal to the insistence on the primacy of freedom for understanding the self as agent in many process philosophers and theologians.

Moreover, the "deprivatizing" of both Catholic and Protestant theologies by the political, liberation, and feminist theologians has also contributed importantly to new Christian prophetic theological reflections on freedom and agency. The insistence on political, economic, and cultural freedom in these theologies has considerably revised any residual purely private or merely individualistic understandings of the self and its freedom. This complex and still developing Christian theological conflict on interpreting freedom can find no easy rehearsal much less resolution here. For

In contrast, see G. R. Evans, *Augustine on Evil* (Cambridge: Cambridge University Press, 1982).

present purposes, it is sufficient to recall some of that history (as above) and to suggest a new way to formulate the question. More exactly, implied in every Christian interpretation of freedom, in the midst of the fierce controversies both within and between Catholic and Protestant theologies as well as within and between more individual-personal understandings of freedom (like Bultmann and Rahner) and more political understandings (like Sölle, Moltmann, Metz, Ruether, Schillebeeckx and Guttierez) is a single refrain for the Christian: the self receives as gift and command the call to freedom. The Christian is a *responsible agent*.[23]

There remains, in all Christian discourse, including the discourse on freedom, what is common even in order to clarify the nature of the differences. The main Christian confession remains "We believe in Jesus the Christ with the apostles." To state the confession as a common confession is, I continue to believe, helpful.[24] For thus stated it clarifies both what Christians are and are not claiming. What they are claiming may be interpreted as follows: how Christians understand the self (and its freedom) as well as history and nature, they understand primarily by their affirmation of Jesus Christ as the decisive manifestation both of who God is and who human beings are empowered and commanded to become. By believing *in* this singular Jesus of Nazareth as the Christ, Christians construe all reality anew in that light: both who God is, how nature and history are ultimately to be understood, and who the self is in its gifted freedom. To eliminate any element of this central confession is to change (sometimes radically, sometimes subtly) the Christian understanding of all reality. For example, the confession is not "We believe in Christ" so that the Sophia-Logos tradition unrelated to the ministry, teaching, death and resurrection of this Jesus of Nazareth confessed to be

---

[23] H. Richard Niebuhr, *The Responsible Self* (New York: Harper & Row, 1963).

[24] See Grant and Tracy, *A Short History of the Interpretation of the Bible*, and David Tracy, *The Analogical Imagination: Christian Theology and the Culture of Pluralism* (New York: Crossroad, 1981), pp. 248-339.

the Christ can suffice. Alternatively, the confession is also not "We believe in Jesus" so that a Jesusology or an alternative portrait of Jesus (e.g., the various quests for the "historical Jesus") can replace the ecclesial Christian confession "We believe in Jesus Christ."

Moreover, the preposition "with" in the phrase "*with* the apostles" cannot be allowed to be replaced by the preposition "in." Then, in effect, the tradition or doctrine or church or apostolic office or text would replace Jesus Christ as that divine reality which the Christian ultimately believes *in*. At the same time, the contemporary Christian believes *in* Jesus Christ *with* the apostles. Aside from the intense inner-Christian debates on what this crucial phrase "with the apostles" means more exactly, this much is shared by Christians: the New Testament texts of the early apostolic communities' witness to Jesus as the Christ are the authoritative texts. As authoritative, those texts are the principal means by which the contemporary Christian's faith in Jesus Christ is tested for its fundamental fidelity to the originating Christian witness to Jesus Christ. Indeed, it may be linguistically preferable to call these texts the "apostolic writings" in order to highlight that the entire New Testament is a text of witness to Jesus Christ by the original "apostolic" communities.

However, to affirm the major role of these texts is also to acknowledge a new Christian hermeneutical question. Where within the pluralism of texts and genres of the New Testament may we find the central Christian construal of this Jesus as The Christ and thereby the Christian construal of God, self, history, and nature? Even the confession "We believe in Jesus Christ with the apostles" is stated, after all, in the genre of confession. The confession is thereby abstracted from the diversity of New Testament christologies in order to affirm the fundamental unity amidst that diversity. The confession, in sum, is a legitimate abstraction from the New Testament, even if it is not an explicitly New Testament confession itself. Nor, for that matter, is confession the principal New Testament genre. Here, as I suggested above, the rediscovery of narrative in contemporary Christian thought shows its true promise — even if in a different way than that envisaged by Hans Frei and other pure "narrativists" in contemporary Christian theology.

For the major genre for the original communities' self-interpretation is gospel — a peculiar genre which unites proclamation, witness, and narrative. Amidst the diversity of narratives within the four gospels and elsewhere in the New Testament, moreover, the passion narratives are the principal ways by which the early Christian community rendered its understanding of who this singular Jesus of Nazareth proclaimed to be the Christ is. It is undoubtedly an exaggeration (but a useful one) to say that the four gospels are four passion narratives with extended and different introductions.[25]

The reason why this statement is an exaggeration is that the different "introductions" are more accurately described as different renderings of the common narrative. There is, to be sure, a notable difference between the genre of apocalpytic drama employed by Mark, the genre of realistic, history-like narrative employed by Luke, and the genre of narrative meditation employed by John. Those genres are not merely taxonomic of meaning but productive of meaning. They provide distinct renderings of the common passion narrative. Still, the reason why this is a useful exaggeration may also be noted. The passion narratives and their relatively history-like, realistic character — despite their otherwise important differences — are the common Christian narratives. If one wants to know who Jesus Christ is for Christians, the passion narratives are the first place to look. For there we find in realistic and history-like fashion the central Christian construal of who this Jesus confessed to be the Christ is and even why he and he alone is thus construed.

Through the rendering of the singular identity of Jesus Christ in the passion narratives, Christians also discover their principal clues to who God is and who human beings as free agents are empowered to become. In sum, as H. Richard Niebuhr long ago

[25] This famous statement is that of Martin Kähler.

discerned,[26] the Christian construal of the self as disclosed in these narratives of Jesus Christ entails a belief in an agent with sufficient freedom to be responsible to God and to others. The Christian, as Christian, needs to affirm the self-as-responsible agent. To be able (and commanded) to respond in and through Christ to God and to neighbor is also to affirm the freedom to be capable of such action. On this foundation, I believe, all the principal Christian theological interpretations of the self and its freedom rest. For despite their otherwise crucial differences on "freedom and grace" or "predestination and freedom" or "bondage of the will," all Christians affirm the reality of a responsible and thereby meaningfully free agent who acts through and in Christ *as* a new authentically free self.

Yet, as the inner-Christian disputes on the exact nature of the freedom of the self of the post-New Testament Christian traditions indicate, there are clearly further questions and further construals of the self's freedom in the Christian tradition. Consider the following list alone: Karl Rahner vs. Karl Barth, Calvinists vs. Arminians, Jansenists vs. Jesuits, Banez vs. Molina, Erasmus vs. Luther, Abelard vs. Bernard of Clairvaux, and, behind them all, the early Augustine vs. the later Augustine. These familiar clashes are intensified in Christian thought by the theological understandings of the prophetic trajectory's further insistence on the social-political character of human freedom before God in the liberation, political, and feminist theologies. It is important to insist that, however conflictual these Christian antagonisms are (and they are), all of them assume three crucial facts: first, there is meaning to the word "freedom" insofar as that word refers to some notion of personal agency and some sense of personal responsibility; second, the ground of that freedom, as Paul insisted, is Jesus Christ; third, the center of that freedom is the kind of agent disclosed by the narratives on the singular agency of this Jesus as the Christ.

---

[26] Niebuhr, *The Responsible Self*. Note how well Niebuhr's responsibility model can be related to the philosophical study of the self by Paul Ricoeur in *Soi-Même comme un autre* (Paris: Editions du Seuil, 1990), pp. 109-199.

To affirm the crucial role of these grounding prophetic narratives on agency (and thereby freedom) in the context of the history of inner-Christian conflict on the agent-as-free is also to note the final problem and promise of inner-Christian understanding of human agency and freedom. The problem is this: the conflict is there from the very beginning of Christian self-interpretation. The problem is there, more exactly, not just in the obvious differences (noted by Luther) between the anthropology of the Letter of James and the Paul of Romans and Galatians. The problem is also there in the different readings of the common passion narrative in the four gospels and even in the abbreviated narrative of Paul of First Corinthians.

Yet this problem yields a promise of differences that may be more like complementarity than sheer conflict. For significantly different readings of the common passion narrative occur in the four gospels. Recall Mark's apocalyptic drama, which, as Frank Kermode justly observes,[27] reads more like a modernist narrative with its interruptions, gaps and fissures, its curious undecidability, its portrait of the disciples' consistent failure to understand, its ultimate non-closure. Contrast this kind of Markan narrative with Luke-Acts whose history-like and realistic character recalls the great nineteenth century realistic narratives of Dickens or Balzac. The situation is even more complex when we note the meditative character of John's narrative:[28] a narrative whose contrasts (light-darkness; truth-falsehood) have a rhythm-like character that give one the impression of hearing an oratorio such as Handel's *Messiah* rather than of reading a realistic or a modernist narrative at all.

In these differences alone, we may find a clue that at least two different readings of the common narrative pervade the New Testament. In general terms, we may name these two readings "prophetic" and "mystical" in the senses outlined earlier in the

---

[27] Frank Kermode, *The Genesis of Secrecy* (Cambridge: Harvard University Press, 1979), pp. 55-63.

[28] Amos Wilder, *The Language of the Gospel: Early Christian Rhetoric* (New York: Harper & Row, 1964), esp. pp. 30-33.

essay on Freud and Lacan. For the moment, it is sufficient to note that any prophetic reading of the gospel highlights the notion of freedom as responsible agency. In our period, that prophetic emphasis is best represented by the insistence on freedom as personal agency and responsibility to the historical struggle of the marginalized and the oppressed in liberation theologies. It finds its more natural New Testament reading in Luke-Acts where the history-like narrative aids the insistence on Jesus' actions for the outcasts of society and the understanding of freedom as not merely private but political as well. It is also true that "when prophecy fails, apocalyptic takes over" — as Mark's apocalyptic drama with its interruptive narrative yielding a construal of history as less continuous than radically discontinuous suggests. Yet even here, as the political theology of J.B. Metz shows,[29] apocalyptic need not mean a retreat from subjecthood and the struggle for freedom in our discontinuous history. Rather apocalyptic can also become, in Mark's use of apocalyptic, an amazing insistence on God as *the* agent in history and, allied to that insight, an equal insistence on the subject as commanded and empowered to act freely even in desperate apocalyptic times.

The alternative reading to the prophetic (or, more fully the prophetic-apocalyptic reading), is equally clear.[30] In the gospel of John a meditative and mystical rereading of the common passion narrative occurs. There one finds a new construal of God-as-love-manifesting-Godself-in *the sign* Jesus Christ and disclosing as well a meditative self empowered and commanded to love. Can a mystic properly read a prophetic text becomes a necessary question for the Christian as soon as one acknowledges John's rereading of the synoptic passion narrative. The same question recurs when the Wisdom tradition and the prophetic traditions

---

[29] Metz, *Faith in History and Society*. See also John Collins, *Apocalyptic as Genre* (Missoula, MT: Semeia, 1978).

[30] The fuller paradigm is prophetic-apocalyptic as distinct from meditative-mystical-archaic. I hope to work out this paradigm for "naming God" in a future book. The paradigm is similar to that of manifestation-proclamation as discussed in *The Analogical Imagination*, pp. 193-231.

give their different readings of the common narratives of the Hebrew Scriptures.

The strong sense of agency (and thereby freedom) of the prophetic reading of the common narrative can sometimes be challenged by the new Johannine model of a loving, meditative self-losing-and-gaining-itself-in-a-new-union-with-the-God-now-construed-as-love in John.[31] Yet such challenge is not discontinuity. As both the neo-Platonist theologies and the classical love-mystics sensed, in John a new sense of freedom-as-love discloses a new possibility for understanding the self as agent. Neither the Christian prophet nor the mystic can live easily with one another. Yet, as the liberation, political, and feminist theologians now insist, only a mystico-prophetic construal of Christian freedom can suffice. Without the prophetic core, the struggle for justice and freedom in the historical-political world can too soon be lost in mere privacy. Without the mystical insistence on love, the spiritual power of the righteous struggle for justice is always in danger of lapsing into mere self-righteousness and spiritual exhaustion.

The question of freedom for the Christian, therefore, is the question of the fuller character of the free agent disclosed by the narrative of Jesus Christ as that narrative is read anew in both prophetic and mystical ways. The "ego" of the purely autonomous modern self with its alluring and illusory freedom is gone. The limited but real freedom of the prophetic-mystical subject-as-agent-in-process has occurred.

It is here that the prophetic thrust of the liberation, political and feminist theologies becomes most clear.[32] For behind the deprivatizing demands of these theologies and behind their insistence on

---

[31] For this tradition in its later "mystical" forms, see the essays by Louis Dupré and Bernard McGinn in Moshe Idel and Bernard McGinn, eds., *Mystical Union and Monotheistic Faith: An Ecumenical Dialogue* (New York: Macmillan, 1989) pp. 3-27 (Dupré) and 59-87 (McGinn).

[32] So clear is this threat that here the more usual designation even for the retrieval of the mystical traditions is "mystical-political." For a representative study here, see Claude Geffré and Gustavo Gutierrez, eds., *The Mystical and Political Dimensions of the Christian Faith, Concilium* 96 (1974).

the priority of praxis over theory, behind their retrieval of the
great suspicions lurking in half-forgotten eschatological symbols
lies their single-minded and constant refrain: Christian theology
must move past both liberal historical consciousness and neo-
orthodox hermeneutical historicity and move again — as Christian theology — into the concrete histories of suffering and
oppression. The great liberation theologies of our day do not
mean by history theories of historiography, or mere philosophies
or theologies of history. They do not mean a purely vertical
transcendence where history becomes a tangent, a theological
accident. With the prophets, the liberation theologians mean
history. They mean the concrete struggles of whole groups,
societies and persons, who have been shunted aside by the official
story of triumph. They mean, with Guttierrez, that the central
theological question today is not the question of the non-believer
but the question of the non-person — the forgotten ones, living
and dead, whose struggle and memory *is* our history.

It is the singular achievement of the liberation and political
theologians that their prophetic, indeed prophetic-mystical, theological return into real history — more exactly into the history of
those whom official historical accounts including Christian theological accounts, have too often disowned as non-persons, non-
groups, non-history: the oppressed, the marginalized, the suffering — now empower these new prophetic-mystical theologies.
That strategy has allowed the liberation, political and feminist
theologians to retrieve in and through their very suspicions of
earlier modern theological interpretations of scripture the repressed moments of the New Testament: the profound negations in
the genre of apocalyptic — so embarrassing to the liberals, so
unnecessary to neo-orthodox eschatologies; the dangerous
memory of Jesus as eschatological prophet — dangerous, above
all, for those who claim his memory as their own.

Here a new hermeneutics of mystical retrieval through prophetic suspicion is clear: the retrieval of the sense of history as
rupture, break, discontinuity in apocalyptic; the retrieval of the

social systemic expression of sin over individual sins; the retrieval of the concrete praxis of discipleship in and for the oppressed.

With the prophets, Christians must ask how is it possible to say we have really entered history — that muddle, that ambiguity, even, at times, with Joyce, that nightmare from which we are attempting to awaken — and not have a prophetic-mystical theology? The alternative is not the theological silence of some mystics on concrete history. This much, however, does seem clear on the contemporary Christian theological horizon: the inter-religious conversation will only become fully serious when the historical events of our century are taken with full theological seriousness. Christian theology will not be the same when that finally occurs. Christian theology in dialogue at last with Jewish thought will then begin to learn the lessons of Jewish thought through the centuries — the lessons of the need for radically new interpretations after radically new interruptive events — the destruction of the Second Temple, the expulsion of Spanish Jewry, and eclipsing them all with its *tremendum* horror and its radically revisionary demands, the Holocaust.[33]

Despite the important revisionary mystico-political work by many Christian theologians in our historical situation, I do not believe that any of us can even guess at the moment where the new Christian theological hermeneutics of both retrieval and suspicion empowered by a new religious mystico-prophetic *via negativa* on both history and nature will eventually lead. Yet this much does seem sure. Those differences will render pale the kind of shifts we are already familiar with. They will prove more radical for Protestant theology than the radical shift that once occurred when the generation of Barth, Tillich, and Bultmann returned from those trenches of World War I where earlier liberal

[33] The import that Jewish thought should bear for Christian theology here should be clear: note the works cited in chapter 3 on the Holocaust. Note, especially, the work of Arthur Cohen, *The Tremendum: A Theological Interpretation of the Holocaust* (New York: Crossroad, 1981); Emil Fackenheim, *The Jewish Return into History* (New York: Schocken, 1978); and the forthcoming book by Susan Shapiro on Jewish responses to the Holocaust.

illusions had collapsed. Those differences will prove more radical for Catholic theology than the kind of sea-change that occurred with later Michelangelo. With Raphael already dead, with the city of Rome ferociously sacked, with the northern Reformation and southern Counter-Reformation crushing the Renaissance Christian humanist hopes of his youth, Michelangelo was forced to abandon the noble dreams of his own youth — the tenderness of the *Pietà*, the classical dignity of *David*, even the tensive triumph of the Sistine Ceiling. Michelangelo turned, for his final vision, to his extraordinary Last Judgment: a judgment where Christ was all judgment, no mercy — judgment upon Christianity itself; a judgment where even the beloved figure of Mary seems to move away from her traditional iconography of tenderness and compassion to fear for humankind. Yet even that classic theological prophetic vision of the Last Judgment — that vision of history as frightening interruption — proved inadequate to Michelangelo. Instead Michelangelo turned again: away from even that clear, firm, and tragic prophetic vision to resign himself and his religious tradition to his final "unfinished" sculptures, his glimpse of a prophetic-mystical way which now beckons so many in the late twentieth century.

Like the kabbalists after the expulsion of Spanish Jewry, like the Protestant neo-orthodox theologians after the War, Michelangelo was willing to take historical events with mystico-prophetic theological seriousness. As the kabbalists still provide some partial analogy for post-Holocaust Jewish thought, past Christian theologies like Michelangelo's can provide some analogy for a contemporary Christian theology struggling to recover and rethink its mystico-prophetic heritage. Every Christian theological hermeneutic today — no matter how powerful and believable its retrievals of its authoritative passion narratives, no matter how fierce and unrelenting its suspicions of the history of the effects of its own readings of those narratives — must now endure as not merely unfinished but as broken. Yet theology is broken only in order to allow for some new beginning of a retrieval of hope. The new theological beginning must this time be in real concrete

history, because it has been chastened by the theological seriousness of the actual history we have witnessed.

As much as Michelangelo, the great artists of the Flemish
Catholic tradition help see our need for both the mystical and the
prophetic with singular clarity. As post-modern Christian thought
recovers a new and healing sense of transience after its welcome
dialogues with Buddhists, the unexampled genius at transience of
Watteau may render that reality for post-modern Christian eyes.
The classical mystical resonances in the great Flemish traditions
of art and thought may help us all to retrieve anew our own half-
forgotten archaic heritage, our own Christian archetypes, and our
own need to recover both Eckhart and Ruysbroeck. Like our
Flemish forebearers, we post-moderns also sense that any serious
retrieval of the classic mystical readings of our prophetic texts
must not retreat from history and the sense of personal and
communal responsibility for the struggle for justice. Any responsible theology today must be what classic Flemish thought, art
and spirituality once exemplified: mystical and prophetic; aesthetic and ethical - political; contemplative and committed to action.

That mystico-political sense of Christian practice and thought,
I believe, may be found with a clarity and power that are
unrivaled not only in the earthy, embodied, worldly mysticism of
the great Flemish tradition but also in the classic Flemish tradition of art. A fine Anglo-American poet, W. H. Auden,[34] caught
that mystico-political sense best perhaps in his poem of reflection
of Flemish art:

Musée des Beaux Arts

About suffering they were never wrong,
The Old Masters: how well they understood
Its human position; how it takes place
While someone else is eating or opening a window or
    just walking dully along!

[34] The poem is to be found in W. H. Auden, Edward Mendelsen, ed., *Collected
Poems* (New York: Random House, 1976).

How, when the aged are reverently, passionately waiting
For the miraculous birth, there always must be
Children who did not specially want it to happen, skating
On a pond at the edge of the wood.

They never forgot
That even the dreadful martyrdom must run its course
Anyhow in a corner, some untidy spot
Where the dogs go on with their doggy life and the
    torturer's horse
Scratches its innocent behind on a tree.

In Brueghel's *Icarus*, for instance: how everything turns
    away
Quite leisurely from the disaster; the ploughman may
Have heard the splash, the forsaken cry.
But for him it was not an important failure; the sun shone
As it had to on the white legs disappearing into the green
Water; and the expensive delicate ship that must have seen
Something amazing, a boy falling out of the sky,
Had somewhere to get to and sailed calmly on.